# Beyond a Dream

## Mark Krebs

*Beyond a Dream Publishing, LLC*

# Beyond a Dream

Cover design by Andrew Krebs
Inside layout by Ad Graphics, Inc.

Printed by Pollock Printing, Nashville, TN

ISBN: 978-0-615-3978-6-3

Published by:
Beyond a Dream Publishing, LLC
415 Licking Pike
Wilder, KY 41071

# Dedication

In memory of my mother, Terri Krebs,
for the strength she possessed and the
inspiration she instilled in so many.
May her spirit live on with the lives
she continues to touch.

# Acknowledgments

Bob Arnold

Clare Bilas

Kip Cornett – Cornett Integrated Marketing Solutions

Katie Fangman

Tom Hoffman – Anderson Realty

Jim Host

Amanda Langferman – Wiley Publishing

Alex Lytle

Rick Mariani

Dudley Webb – Webb Companies

# Table of Contents

# Foreword

## By John Calipari
## June 2010

In my first year as coach at the University of Kentucky there were many milestones and memories that will stay with me a lifetime. As a whole, the team won 35 games – including the regular and post-season SEC crowns – and advanced to the Elite 8 of the NCAA Tournament. Off the court, we impacted the community in a multitude of ways, highlighted by our Hoops for Haiti telethon, which helped raise $1.5 million for relief efforts in earthquake-ravaged Haiti.

It was, in every sense of the word, an incredible first season as the head coach at college basketball's all-time winningest program.

But there is one moment that I will carry with me for as long as I walk on this earth. It occurred during our Senior Day ceremonies on March 7, 2010 at Rupp Arena just before we tipped off against Florida in our regular season finale. Our four graduating players – Ramon Harris, Mark Krebs, Patrick Patterson and Perry Stevenson – were introduced and congregated at center court to be saluted by our fans in the annual tradition of Senior Day.

As Mark joined his family, he bent down to his mom, Terri, in her wheelchair and gave her a hug and a kiss. Two days shy of her 49th birthday, Terri had been waging a courageous eight-year battle against breast cancer. When she was first diagnosed, doctors gave her less than a year to live. On that Sunday in our historic arena, Terri Krebs proved to all of the Big Blue Nation what perseverance, positivity and probably most of all, LOVE, can do for a person.

After Mark had embraced his mom, the three other players and their parents went over and hugged Terri as well; the rest of our players followed their lead. It was a few minutes before game time and I found myself, like many in the building, trying to hold back the tears.

When you see something like that and are a part of it, it kind of kicks you right in the gut. It tends to put everything in perspective.

It meant so much to our program to be able to share Senior Day 2010 with Mark and his family. Likewise, it meant a lot to me to be able to coach Mark in his final season as a Wildcat.

When I arrived in Lexington in the spring of 2009, there were a lot of decisions that had to be made. From staff hires to scheduling to decorating our offices, the list was long and involved. There were no more difficult decisions than the ones regarding players we had inherited from the previous coaching staff. One of my first priorities when we got to campus was to sit down with all the returning players and explain what would be expected of them and how they might expect to be used in our system.

Some of the players were enthused about the new start they were about to get; others were concerned about their roles and decided to leave the program. And then there was Mark.

He had been a walk-on for the previous three years and all the reports I had received on Mark indicated that he was a great kid, a superb student and a respected leader. When we first spoke I was immediately struck by Mark's maturity, his passion for the game and his enthusiastic attitude. He told me how meaningful it had been for him to be part of the program he grew up watching and adoring. He explained that he saw his role as a "do-anything" type of guy. He knew that playing time would be scarce, practices would be long and the expectations for each player were being raised a few notches.

"Are you willing to accept that role?" I asked him.

"Without a doubt," he said. "Whatever you need from me, I'll do."

I was, to say the least, impressed by Mark. With one available scholarship, our staff decided there was no one more deserving than Mark. We had all taken note of his passion for the game from day one and we knew he would help provide senior leadership to an inexperienced team. On top of all that, Mark was really an exceptional Division I player. He could shoot, defend and run an offense effectively – he was not your typical former "walk-on." He could have played at a lot of excellent programs.

In the pre-season, when we were trying to figure out our personnel and experimenting with different line-ups, I was never hesitant to put Mark in the game. I knew he could handle any situation. In fact, he was so steady and so intuitive on the court that I took to calling his impact on those early games and practices, "The Krebs Effect."

It's funny now that I think back on those words. I was originally talking about the effect Mark had on the floor in making our other guys better through his hustle and feel for the game.

Looking back, I now realize that "The Krebs Effect" was something much more for our program and our fans. Mark showed all of us the importance of family and being there for his mom. He never complained and never used Terri's sickness as an excuse. He just went about his daily work and made himself and his teammates better each and every day. More than just teammates, Mark leaves our program with brothers who would do anything for the Krebs family.

It was meaningful to all of us to be able to share Mark's final season in college and I am honored to be able to provide this foreword for his inspirational and worthy book. The message Mark delivers is similar in many ways to the theme of my recent book, Bounce Back. There is no roadmap for dealing with a loved one's sickness and likewise there is no GPS to instruct young men on living life to its fullest. Mark's inspiring final season at UK shows each of us how precious our days on Earth are and how meaningful they can become for others.

Mark's story – and that of Terri – are the type that are too often overlooked or given short shrift. By sharing his ups, downs and in-betweens with readers, Mark is defining exactly what "The Krebs Effect" is all about.

# 1

# FOUNDATION:
## It all Starts with Family

The final buzzer sounded. I looked up at the scoreboard to see the final score: University of Kentucky 66, West Virginia University 73. Sadly, our 2010 NCAA Tournament run had come to a screeching halt. As a #1 seed, we were upset by #2 West Virginia, and the National Championship we had worked for all year long was ripped from our grasp. As I walked off the floor of the Carrier Dome after the Elite Eight in Syracuse, a flood of overwhelming emotion crashed down on me. For the first time in four years, I felt lost, lonely, and dejected.

In the locker room, I almost couldn't bring myself to take off my jersey for the last time. It gave me a sick, gut-wrenching feeling just thinking about it. The memories flew through my head. I sat looking around the locker room, taking in the reactions of all my teammates and brothers...finally realizing the journey was over.

Fighting back tears, I thought about my years as a Kentucky Wildcat. My senior season had come to a heart-rending close, and I found it worthwhile to look back at all that had happened. I lived every day in admiration of my mom's courageous fight with breast cancer; made the improbable rise from a small Division III college to the Mecca of college basketball; and proved myself to three coaches in four years, eventually earning a scholarship after playing three years as a walk-on.

## We can't always explain why certain situations happen

There is no doubt in my mind that all of these things happened for a reason. The hand I was dealt never felt like a burden – just obstacles on the way to reaching my dreams. Gazing at my past now fills me with inspiration and hope for a bright future.

Don't get me wrong; every single person throughout the world has their own unique circumstances, and some are worse than others. Sometimes, just like my story, there's no rhyme or reason to the madness. But many times, it's the way people react to the adversity that means the most. We can't always explain why certain situations happen, but much can be said about how we deal with them.

As I sat in the locker room thinking back through my life, it was plain to see that even at birth, adversity was no stranger. Although neither of us knew it at the time, my mother and I would share a unique bond throughout life.

• • •

I was born on October 10, 1986, as a new addition to a family of three: a mother, a father, and an older sister. As is true with everyone, I don't remember my actual birth, but I have been given numerous accounts of what transpired on that October day.

My parents both speak of the joy and pride they possessed as they held their newborn son. It was the same excitement they had experienced a few years earlier when my older sister, Amanda Marie, was born on December 22, 1982.

Shortly after my birth, their expressions of joy and pride changed to concern when the doctor entered the room and explained to them that their baby boy would need to be placed under a bilirubin lamp because of my jaundiced condition. Jaundice is rated by doctors and nurses with a number; above 10 isn't normal. Babies can be placed under lamps that help to break up the excess bilirubin in their skin. My number happened to be slightly above 10.

As a result of the circumstances, the two stories I hear most about my very early childhood come from my mother and my father and focus on the initial moments of my life. My parents both have their own favorite tales they love to tell.

My father's favorite revolves around how he personally saved my life and is responsible for my survival during those initial days. He mentions the jaundice event but says there was also a brief mention of an x-ray that showed some fluid around my kidneys. My parents were told that that fluid was of no concern and would simply flush out of my system.

After a few days, near my release from the hospital, my dad asked the doctor, "Do you know anything about the fluid build up in my son's kidneys? Is that ok now? It was pointed out by one of the nurses while he was still in the nursery."

The physician replied, "I am unaware of any fluid around the kidneys; in fact, this is the first I have ever heard of it. Since there is a bit of concern, we should take another x-ray to double-check."

To my parent's horror, they found that the fluid was still there, and in fact, had accumulated to a significantly concerning level.

The release from the hospital was retracted so further testing could be performed on me. Results showed that the urethra was being crushed, thereby stopping fluid from leaving the body normally. Amazingly, my parents were told I wouldn't have survived if we'd left the hospital and headed home that day. The situation was so serious that immediate surgery was required to repair the urethra. Thanks to my dad's unyielding persistence, I survived the near-tragic ordeal.

This leads into my mom's story. It focuses on how no matter where I was during those first moments of my life, my eyes would scan the room looking for her face.

One particular instance occurred when I was due back for another kidney surgery a few months after being born. My mom explains how hard it was to see me in the recovery room after surgery and emphatically stated that no matter what was going on with me or around me, I could pick her out in a crowd in a second and was always doing my best to search for her. Once I spotted her, my eyes would lock on her. She says that gave her comfort and a peaceful feeling inside.

Although I've heard those two stories many times over the years, I don't need them to remind me of my traumatic beginnings in life. I have a constant, more physical reminder of my kidney surgery in the scar on the left side of my lower back. It's truly remarkable that as my body grows, the scar grows with it, and, like most boys, ever since my youth, I've worn the scar with pride. Whenever people would ask about the scar, I wouldn't go into details of the surgery. It was more fun to simply say it was from a knife fight or a shark attack.

Nevertheless, despite how much I enjoyed having a "cool" scar to show all the kids at school, life at home was tough during my first few weeks and months. It was difficult for my parents to care for a 4-year-old daughter while frequently taking me back to the hospital to make sure my kidneys were still working properly, but that didn't bother them in the least. Regardless of how taxing the duties were on my parents, they were just glad I was living at home and out of the hospital.

To get a grasp on what my early childhood was like, I always think back to stories my family shared with me as I was growing up. I believe it's the only way we can get a picture of what life was like back when we were little.

The way I see it, my childhood must have been chaos because my family never had a shortage of entertaining stories to tell. Whether the stories fill me with uncontrollable laughter or make me weep with sadness, they all, in some way, define me.

For example, I was only two years old when my mom's mother, my Grandma Marie, passed away. At the young age of 57, my grandmother lost her life because of an aneurysm to the aorta in her heart. She left this earth without warning.

My parents always tell me the bittersweet story of how I kept my grandfather distracted during the funeral. No matter how sad the mood became or how much crying there was, I kept running back into his arms after he would let me down, forcing him to hold me again.

He later told my mom that my constant hand holding and hugs helped him get through it. It took his mind off death and brought it back to thinking about life. Without realizing it then, I made him smile and played a positive role in helping him and the rest of my family make it through the tragic loss.

That story has a bit of foreshadowing in it, now that I think about it. Throughout life, I have always been the one to lighten up the mood or brighten a gloomy situation. As far back as my memory will go, seeing people smile and laugh never ceased to put me in good spirits. The thought of crying very rarely entered my mind. Unfortunately, I didn't realize how much sadness would eventually flood into my life in the future.

---

Back in the locker room on that cold night in Syracuse, NY., there was no way to raise everyone's spirits. The ache of defeat was too much to handle. I looked over to John, Demarcus, and Patrick, along with many of the others, and realized this was our last game for Kentucky. We would never get these moments back.

I began to think about all the venues, cities, and countries that basketball allowed me to visit over the years. How did a kid from Newport, Ky. end up in the Carrier Dome for an Elite Eight game in the NCAA Tournament? What started me on this path? These questions inevitably led me back to my childhood.

• • •

Newport, Ky. was a wonderful place to grow up in. It was the birthplace of both my parents and is considered part of the Greater Cincinnati area, lying just south of Cincinnati across the Ohio River. We jokingly call Cincinnati one of our suburbs.

Our house on Observation Avenue in Newport was truly a child's paradise. Our house sat at the bottom of a long and winding dead-end street. It was a street full of children our age who all seemed to gather at our place. Dad kept the cars parked in the driveway so that the garage could be a playroom for us. There was a huge deck on the back of the house, which was surrounded by woods.

Not a day went by when we weren't playing wiffleball in the front yard or my big sister Mandy wasn't out of control on her bike running through the driveway and down into the woods. She would be screaming the whole way down as branches and limbs broke with every rotation of the tires. Mandy would exit the woods with bike in hand, hair covered in twigs, and I would be there to meet her with unstoppable laughter.

My early years were filled with many hilarious moments and entertaining encounters like this one. I was fortunate to be blessed with an amazing family that enjoyed each other's company. And the real beauty was things would only get better.

On May 24th, 1991, my younger brother, Andrew Douglas, was born. Knowing the responsibility that was ahead of me, I was ready to be a big brother and role model for Andrew.

However, now with three kids in the family, my mother made the decision to quit her job at ITT Finance. At the time, Mandy was in elementary school, I was 4 and would soon be getting ready for kindergarten and 1st grade, and Andrew was a newborn.

Without work, she began babysitting all my cousins and a few other children, mostly children of family friends. My mom basically made a business out of it, while also having the joy of being home with her children. This only meant one thing to me at the time: a house full of other kids to play with every single day.

Personally, the prospect of having company everyday intrigued me because I didn't usually have other boys to play with around the house. Mandy was great, but she was beginning to play unfair. She wanted me to join in the fun and games around the house, but unfortunately, that fun usually involved playing with Barbie dolls. She talked me into letting her dress me up like a girl in frilly clothes. Not knowing any different when she laughed, I thought we were just having fun. But once it became clear she was using me for her amusement, I began to hide out.

While in hiding, I would look for my dad and hang out with him. It was necessary for me to know what he was doing and if he needed help. As a result, my dad and I became very close, very early.

———————

Looking back at my past didn't take the sting out of playing the final game of my college basketball career, but before I could move forward with life, I knew I had to appreciate where I had already been.

After spending a few moments with tears in my eyes and gazing back in time, Coach Calipari did his best to rally the troops after such a crushing defeat. He took awhile before delivering the last post-game speech I would ever hear. He did everything he could to be enthusiastic, but the circumstances were too tough. It reminded me of my father speaking to my grade school teams after what seemed like the toughest loss we had ever experienced.

As I listened to the words Coach Cal spoke to the team, it took every ounce of discipline to keep my mind from wondering back to when I was little. Realizing that this was the conclusion of my playing days at Kentucky, my mind drifted all the way back to the very beginning of sports for me.

• • •

In 1977, after college graduation, Dad became a high school teacher and an assistant basketball coach at his alma mater, Newport Catholic High School. After coaching freshman and JV for a while, he took over the reigns as head coach of the varsity team. It was interesting to know my dad as Coach Krebs during the earlier years, but I liked it.

It was because of my dad's love for basketball that the sport became infused in my blood at a very early age. He never forced basketball on me, but it was something in which I immediately took an interest. It seemed I could never get enough of the game; I would spend countless hours following my dad to the gym for his team's practices.

He became my coach, mentor, and best friend early in my development. At 3:00 every afternoon, I would go directly to the high school gymnasium where I got to hang out with my dad, give water to the players, and shoot on the side hoops during practice. At the age of 5, I was making three-pointers, which always seemed to impress people who entered the gym during Newport's practices.

I learned a great deal about basketball and life from my dad. He was full of unusual quirks and a never-ending sense of humor, but one undeniable truth was that he loved his children.

One of the earliest memories I have of my father and his compassion took place at his softball game when I was 5. My dad played on a team full of friends and family, including my mom's brothers, my Uncle Joe and Uncle Wayne, two or three times a week. Mom would always drag Mandy, Andrew, and me to the games. We didn't mind too much because we got to play with our cousins and the other players' children during the hot summer weekends.

Before I continue this story, I should note that at this point in my life, I had already developed the habit of always sticking my tongue out when I had the ball just like "Mike." (Of course, I'm referring to my basketball hero, Michael Jordan. You may have heard of him?) Being obsessed, I watched every game he played. Since MJ dribbled and shot with his tongue out, it was necessary that I do the same.

When my dad's softball game was over, everyone gathered at the playground. It seemed like a perfect time to show off how high I could jump. Proving to my family that I could jump off the top platform of the swing set was no small feat. After all, the platform was about 10 feet high, and I was only 5 years old at the time.

Despite some people's warnings that I could get hurt, I proceeded to jump up as high as possible off the top of the platform. Feeling like "Mike," I glided to the ground with my hands up and tongue out. I stuck the landing like a gymnast going for gold. Unfortunately, however, the force of the landing made me chomp my teeth down and practically bite off my tongue. It hung on by only a few strands of flesh. A quick realization of not being invincible rushed through me. It was the worst pain I had ever experienced.

My tongue dangled as an immediate puddle of blood gathered at my feet. Mom and Dad acted quickly to try and keep what was left of my tongue in my mouth as they sped off to the emergency room. My mother stuffed napkins and a handkerchief into my mouth to soak up the blood during the ride to the hospital. The pain was excruciating.

Once in the emergency room, we had to sit and wait while my parents completed the usual paperwork. My mind was racing. How do they reattach a tongue? Will I ever talk normally again?

The tears rushed down my cheeks like rain.

It was at this point that my dad looked over at me and said, "Come on, shake it off, it's not that big of a deal. You just bit your tongue a little. When I was your age, I used to bite my tongue off three times a week. You're not a man until you bite off your tongue."

This honestly shows the type of man my dad is. On the outside, his compassion doesn't come in the form of sympathy or pity.

Whenever you're hurt, he sends a token of encouragement, "Shake it off, don't worry about it, dust yourself off, pick up, and move on. You're going to be just fine."

My tears subsided with the comforting words of my dad and the realization that he'd gone through the same thing when he was little. The doctor called us in moments later and assured me they could fix my tongue with no problem. I was lucky everything was normal again after a few peroxide treatments. It's truly amazing how fast the tongue heals; by the time elementary school started, I was as good as new.

When I first started school at St. Therese Elementary, I was put in an instructional basketball league with other children my age. It wasn't the setup of choice, considering I already knew the rules and skills of the game, thanks to all the time I spent in the gym growing up. And even though my dad knew the instructional league was boring for me, he encouraged me to stick with it because of the friendships I would make. He ended up leveling with me and arranged for me to play on teams with the 3rd and 4th graders because he believed I could compete with them even in the 1st and 2nd grades.

After starting out in the instructional leagues and on teams my dad got me on with the older kids, I moved on to play AAU basketball also. In the 4th grade, I played for the 5th grade and under team. All we did was win, all season long. One of the biggest games of my youth was one of those AAU games. As an undefeated team, we were searching for a state championship and a birth to nationals.

I remember the state final game like it was yesterday. We played a team called the Knicks. They had all the gear: bags and uniforms with their names and numbers printed on the sides as if Nike sponsored them. Basically, they had all the things that AAU teams have today but no one had back then. It was intimidating to say the least. The Knicks strolled into the gym wearing sunglasses and shouldering all the confidence in the world. They seemed unstoppable. Coach O'Hara, my AAU coach growing up, reminded us to play our game and not be intimidated.

He said, "Remember the fundamentals, play good defense, and make sure everyone is having fun. Let's play our game, and we will win."

Suddenly the spiffy uniforms they were wearing, the monogrammed gear they possessed, and their arrogant attitude no longer gave them the psychological edge. We knew we had a great coach who knew what we needed in order to win. We were going to heed his words, play our game, and not worry about the other team.

The game went back and forth; the lead kept changing from one team to the other. It was destined to be a great finish, a game that would come down to the wire. The scoreboard showed that the Knicks were up by one point. With ten seconds to play, we had possession. The ball was brought past half court and thrown to me. The game rested in my hands.

The clock showed four seconds left as I drove to the middle of the lane and shot the game-deciding jumper. The ball hit the rim with a clang, bounced high in air, and fell to the court. I thought we had lost the game, but before I had time to react, the whistle blew. Luckily, the referee had called a foul.

I had to make one free throw to tie the game and two to win. The referee who called the foul was Dicky Beal, a former star guard for the University of Kentucky from 1980 through 1984. All of us Kentuckians knew who he was.

The Knicks called a timeout to try and ice me. Referee Beal came over to me as I stood at the foul line.

He handed me the ball and said, "Hey kid, you aren't nervous now are you?"

I replied, "No sir," and I did my usual routine: dribbled the ball three times, took a deep breath, kept my eyes focused intently on the rim, and shot.

The first one went in, nothing but net. The crowd cheered as I had just tied the game. The Knicks called another timeout, and back onto the ice I went.

When the timeout ended, Referee Beal was back at it again, "You sure you aren't nervous? You know this is to win the game."

I remembered what my dad had taught me in my early days about foul shooting – the routine, the concentration, and the focus.

Looking up at the ref, I coolly replied again, "No sir."

I focused, dribbled three times, took a deep breath, focused on the rim, and released the ball. It felt good the moment it left my hands. It seemed to move in slow motion as I followed it through the air intently. It was my time to shine. Every boy's dream is to be the hero of a game. This was finally my chance to help keep our team on the path for nationals. Would all the time I spent practicing foul shots actually pay off?

The answer was an enthusiastic yes – nothing but net! We won the game and were headed to nationals!

In all honesty, that AAU game was the first time I really wanted to win. Thinking back on it, this was the first time I hungered to succeed in sports and the first time there was a promise of being a real "player." Granted, I was just an extremely skinny kid with the drive to be an athlete; after that game, though, I was an athlete who had the drive to be a winner.

We won the state championship that year, and our team continued the winning streak for three straight years. Even though I was only a small kid, events like that first big AAU game slowly molded my thoughts and actions. They made me think like an athlete and not just a kid leisurely playing sports. I quickly learned the value of devoting my time and effort to something. That game laid the groundwork for my realizing the rest of my potential.

———

Thirty minutes after the final horn sounded to end the last game of my career, I still couldn't take off my jersey. I remembered putting my Kentucky uniform on for the first time, and it made me cry harder. I could picture the uniform hanging neatly in my locker at Rupp Arena with *Kentucky* across the front, *Krebs* on the back, and the number 12 right below it.

Even the sights and sounds of my childhood remained vivid in my memory. As a matter of fact, it seemed like only yesterday that I was suited up for my AAU team, standing at the free throw line, ready to send our team to nationals. People always say it, but life really does fly by.

• • •

Those early years of elementary school seemed to move so fast. Life itself was moving at such a rapid pace, especially for my parents. With us three kids playing sports, my dad realized that his high school coaching was taking up all of his time. Because he was missing us grow up, he elected to walk away from coaching. He resigned as head coach after twenty years on the sidelines.

I really respect that decision and will always appreciate the sacrifice he made for us. His high school coaching days came to an end, but when one door closes another one opens. He now had the opportunity to coach Mandy, Andrew, and me. From 5th grade until 8th grade, he would be a part of every coaching staff of mine, and it was crucial to my development.

> It's a belief of mine that we become a cumulative result of our experiences

It took some time to realize, but all of these memories with my family helped form a foundation for who I would become in the years to follow. An early childhood full of love and excitement shaped me as an individual. Even the years of Mom's babysitting taught me how to share and socialize with other kids. It's a belief of mine that we become a cumulative result of our experiences. The people around us as we grow up impact our lives forever, and my parents, along with my entire family, made my childhood experiences priceless.

# 2

# CONFIDENCE:

## The Calm before the Storm

As I progressed through the 6th, 7th, and 8th grades, I quickly began to realize that although I was still a kid, it was time to be responsible and more mature. New experiences were going to flood my life during this period, so I had to be ready.

Good old puberty was kicking in and, with it, came awkwardness, clumsiness, and goofiness. Because of my rapid growth, my body didn't have time to catch up. No matter what I tried, weight would not stick to my skinny frame. It was a bitter truth to come to grips with, but during my middle school years, lanky and gawky were the words that best described me. It was a rough couple of years in the appearance category, to say the least.

Home life, on the other hand, couldn't have been better. Mandy was enjoying high school at Newport Central Catholic; Andrew and I still attended St. Therese; my dad was still teaching history at Newport Independent High School; and Mom's babysitting business couldn't have been doing better. Best of all, Dad was still able to focus on coaching us kids. He was enjoying the transition into spending more time with his family since he'd given up coaching high school basketball.

• • •

In middle school, the 7th grade to be exact, my illustrious baseball career came to an end. I had a good run, but it was time to say good-bye. Baseball never actually felt like my sport. I'm a firm believer that if you have a good experience with something, you'll come back to it time and time again. Likewise, if you have a few disastrous moments with something, you aren't likely to want to continue that venture. Baseball was like that for me. There were more than a few unfortunate moments while participating in America's favorite pastime.

I vividly remember one such moment that occurred during a baseball practice. Dad was out of town, so Mom was left with the task of taking Andrew and me to all of our sporting events. She drove to the baseball field for my weekly practice and was in a rush to take Andrew to his game at another ballpark. Once they dropped me off and began to pull away, Andrew noticed my forgotten batting gloves lying on the seat. He quickly hopped out of the van and ran to deliver the gloves.

Meanwhile, my team took the field and was eager to begin the evening's practice.

As Andrew made his jaunt back to our brand new mini-van, Mom honked the horn to hurry him up because she was blocking the entrance to the parking lot. When 7-year-old Andrew was getting back in the van, his baseball cleats slipped off the metal foothold, causing him to fall while trying to jump in the van. Mom, frustrated at the cars beeping at her to move, thought he was in the van and had slammed the door shut behind him.

Unfortunately, that wasn't the case at all. My mom pressed on the gas just enough to move out of the way of the entrance. His grip on the door handle was too weak for the sudden movement of the vehicle as he fell from the moving car. My mom, who thought Andrew was safely buckled into his seat, saw her youngest son tumbling head over feet down the pavement behind her. The tires grazed his flesh and his head flung violently onto the concrete.

My teammate yelled to me from third base, "Mark, your Mom just ran over Andrew."

In the parking lot, Andrew lay motionless fifteen feet behind our van. I gasped as my heart jumped out of my chest. My glove dropped to the dirt. I ran as quickly as possible, along with what seemed like great masses of children, players, and parents, to my little brother.

Someone called the life squad and a voice from the crowd yelled, "The ambulance has been called. They are nearby and will be here shortly."

To me, it was just background noise as my focus was strongly on Andrew and my mom, who stood there shocked. Words couldn't even escape her lips.

The scariest part was this: Andrew stood up. He didn't answer anyone's questions. He looked at Mom, then at me, and then, without warning, his eyes rolled in the back of his head as he fainted back to the ground.

The ambulance came and rushed him to the hospital. My mom of course jumped in with him, and Mandy met them at the hospital. Since she was afraid I was traumatized or something, Mom assured me everything was okay and insisted I get back to practice.

In the end, Andrew was all right. The door had slammed back and broke a few of his ribs, the tires grazed him, and his head hit the pavement with such force it caused a crack in his skull, but other than that, he was good as new. Even though she didn't exactly run over him, Mom was terribly upset about what had happened. She was angry at her impatience and carelessness.

I tried my best to make her feel better, but it was upsetting to me, too. If I hadn't forgotten my batting gloves, none of this would've happened. Now my brother had to stay overnight in the hospital for observation because of his head injury, and my mom had to make the dreadful call to Dad.

He was in Florida when he received the telephone call from Mom pleading, "Don't panic. Andrew is in the hospital, but he is fine. I sort of ran over him today." Who knows what he was thinking at the time?

Soon after Andrew was released from the hospital, my parents took him on a shopping spree at the toy store.

My uncle brought light and humor to the situation days after the accident when he shouted to all the kids at one of our family gatherings, "Go take a ride with Terri if you want new toys."

Even Mom had to laugh at that.

• • •

Another ill-fated baseball mishap of mine happened one summer at the conclusion of my dad's summer recreation camp. It was a camp that he ran during the summer months that kids from all over the area would come to and play sports all day long. Of course, the main activity for the entire camp was baseball.

Since it was a rainy day, the actual baseball field was muddy and off limits. My dad decided to set up the bases and make a field across the outside basketball courts. Sometime after our game started, I remember running after a high fly ball, wanting desperately to make the game winning catch. Willie Mays style, I looked backward over my shoulder, saw the ball, and ran it down full speed. My eyes made contact with the basketball pole a moment before I ran smack-dab into it. Everything went dark.

I regained consciousness in time to feel soft slaps against my face to wake me up. It was my dad making sure I wasn't dead. I was still alive, but most of my front teeth were knocked out. An enormous lump appeared instantly on my forehead, and my kneecap was just as swollen as my forehead. My entire body was a mess.

As he picked me up to carry me to the car, my dad's compassion once again shined bright as he yelled, "You're such a cute kid. Why do you do stuff like this to your face."

He yelled this as if running into a concrete basketball structure was enjoyable for me. It was clear he was just nervous at the sight of me fainting and the huge egg-like swelling that was forming on my forehead.

As soon as we got into the car, my Dad drove directly to the hospital to make sure everything checked out. I was free to go home and was assured that the swelling would go down in time. The question was when; I was beginning to look a lot like a Klingon from Star Trek. Luckily, one of my cousins was a dentist, so at least I got my teeth fixed the same day.

• • •

After these events, I quickly realized that my future in baseball was limited. So I decided to give up baseball to concentrate on other sports, like football, golf, and most importantly, basketball. With my dad as a former coach, basketball was always my true sport. Without the break from baseball, I wouldn't have been able to focus on my other three sports. The opportunity to play in more golf tournaments and attend as many basketball camps as possible took its place.

Without a doubt, the basketball camps I attended between the ages of 12 and 16 were vital to my growth as an athlete, and my approach and positive outlook toward them helped make them all the more beneficial. I developed my attitude and philosophy toward sports at an early age, and they stayed with me throughout my years as an athlete.

My dad mentored me and taught me how to optimize the camp experience. He encouraged me to go to each camp with one overarching goal in mind: to learn from coaches who knew the sport.

He would always tell me, "Don't just *hear* what they're saying; *listen* to what they're saying. When the camp is over, remember the drills they taught you and, through practice, you will get better. It's impossible to get better in only a week of camp."

I would return home from camp and practice the drills all summer long; when the school year began, the change was noticeable. It wasn't long before I started to develop confidence in my skills. Thanks to this confidence and my years of hard work, I was in position to excel when I entered high school at a small school with a rich tradition called Newport Central Catholic (a.k.a. NewCath).

In the 8th grade, NewCath played in a team camp at Eastern Kentucky University. They invited me to travel with the JV and Varsity teams to play in the camp. This camp was not only a chance for me to prove myself at a higher level but also an opportunity to show Mr. Detzel, my future high school coach, what I had to offer as a player.

I had wanted to play at NewCath since grade school. It was a place that was a part of my makeup as a kid. One of the top players in NBA history, Dave Cowens, the great Boston Celtic, went there. It was also where my dad played and coached for years before moving to the public high school in Newport.

I distinctly remember following the NewCath Thoroughbreds closely throughout my middle school years. I remember going to the 2000 Kentucky Sweet Sixteen High School Tournament to root them on in Lexington. I remember the excitement in the air when I entered the city.

Although college – and high school – basketball is a pretty huge deal in Kentucky and although Rupp Arena is sacred ground to many fans, I had never been there before the 2000 state high school tournament. Making the walk to the massive building from the parking lot, I can remember thinking about all the Kentucky greats that stepped foot in that building. The history behind it filled my mind, and I could feel the tradition as I entered Rupp Arena for the first time. It was electric. Imagining how it would look filled with 23,000 screaming fans for a UK game gave me the chills. Someday I wanted to be there but not as a spectator or fan.

From that day on, my goal became to strive everyday to make it to Rupp Arena for the state high school championship. That same day, I became captivated by visions of being there in uniform as a UK player, and as a result, set out to achieve another, farther reaching goal – to live out every Kentucky boy's dream of playing for the Kentucky Wildcats.

• • •

Before that could happen, though, I had to make the big transition from middle school to the high school. I remember feeling at ease because my life, in the short term, was mapped out. I would attend NewCath, enjoy high school, and excel on the basketball court. The rest was history.

Fretting over grades was never a problem for me because schooling always came first. My dad was a teacher, and my mom was strict and demanding, to say the least. Only our very best effort was acceptable. All I had to worry about was preparing for the challenges of competing athletically at the high school level and, of course, keeping up with chores around the house.

Despite having fourteen kids at a time running around the house, my mom kept the house tidy. She would clean the house twice a day even when babysitting so many kids. Needless to say, our home was spotless. My mom was stern but also loving, caring, and giving. She was always there to listen to our stories and give us advice. She loved babysitting kids and played with them for hours. Among her favorite tasks were reading to them, telling stories, and teaching how to share.

As her children, we were obviously held to higher standards. It was vital to clean up after ourselves, put plates in the dishwasher after we ate, make our beds each morning, put clothes away in the hamper if dirty or on hangers and in drawers if clean. We always had to put toys away properly after playing with them, and homework always had to be done immediately after school.

At times, the never-ending demands wore on me, but I now know that those

## ...those chores molded me into the person I am today

chores molded me into the person I am today. We were a normal family with loving, caring parents, who brought us up properly in every aspect of the word. Looking back on those times in my life, a smile forms because I now understand the importance of them.

• • •

The way I remember it, our lives were setting up perfectly during my middle school years. We had just moved into our new house after living in a duplex for two years while the house was being built.

Inevitably, with a family of five, living quarters were pretty tight in the duplex for those two years, but we managed. The duplex had a kitchen, a living room with a bright orange shag carpet, my parent's bedroom, and a second bedroom that all three children shared. All the rooms were quite small, and everyone had to share one bathroom. It was difficult at times, but just like anything, we found fun in it. We got along with each other and understood sharing was the only way to survive. Even though we endured the tight quarters and found enjoyment in the conditions, we were certainly excited about the new house.

Once we settled into our new home in Newport, it was truly unbelievable to us. We had a nice yard in a new subdivision, three bedrooms, and a large basement. The living room, dining room, and kitchen were the perfect size for our family. Sharing a room with Andrew was still a must, but it was big enough for the both of us. Finally, I had a room to freely decorate any way my heart desired (as long as it was okay with Andrew, of course).

The best part was that Mom and Dad thought the house would be more complete if we added another member to the family. The next day, we all went out and picked up our new sister, Nala, a beautiful golden retriever puppy.

The house and neighborhood were everything we needed. I had grade school friends as neighbors to build tree houses with in the woods, play baseball with in the street, and shoot basketball with in the driveway. Every day was an adventure for me. It was incredible.

We finally had everything we wanted and needed. Knowing that my future was set for NewCath and that basketball was finally coming together filled me with confidence. Plus, we had our health, a strong family, friends, and a brand new dog. Life was good for the Krebs family.

> We finally had everything we wanted and needed

# 3

# ADVERSITY:
## Life in the Face of Devastation

The start of high school meant maximum excitement for me. Meeting new friends, being with the old pals I'd grown up with, and playing sports at Newport Central Catholic were unexplainable joys. November brought the end of my freshman football season with a record of 8 wins and 0 losses. As the starting quarterback on an undefeated team, things were looking up for me.

After football season, all my attention and excitement turned to the start of the long-awaited basketball season. The anticipation for it to get underway was mounting. After all, I'd been envisioning this moment for years. All the practices, basketball camps, and sacrifices I'd made put me in the position to start my high school basketball career on the right foot.

But what waited at home for me the afternoon of my first high school basketball game was bigger than the kickoff of my new career. It was bigger than anything I could've ever expected. As a freshman in high school, my world was about to crumble.

• • •

It was a beautiful Friday afternoon, and thoughts of the upcoming game made it nearly impossible to get through the school day. I rushed home filled with excitement and anticipation.

After being dropped off in front of the house, I noticed things were different than most days. Our driveway and street were filled with cars, and I recognized each of them. They were the cars of my mom's entire side of the family. Immediate concern set in.

Why were they here on a Friday afternoon? Why did they all take off work early?

I cautiously opened the front door. After scanning the room, my heart stopped, and an ill feeling filled my stomach. A wave of devastating emotion filled the house as my entire family sat weeping with looks of hopelessness on their faces. I saw my Aunt Joyce, the oldest of the Seibert family, first. Tears were running down her cheeks.

## Without anyone saying a word, I knew she'd been diagnosed with breast cancer

I continued to look around the living room at a multitude of somber expressions. Andrew, Mandy, and my dad all had the look of despair painted heavily on their faces. It was clear something terrible had happened.

Hoping for a small bit of comfort, my eyes immediately focused on my mom. Sadly, I didn't find any hope in her face; she was crying most of all.

It came to me at once; this was the day she was getting her test results back. Without anyone saying a word, I knew she'd been diagnosed with breast cancer.

• • •

After much deliberation, I decided to play in the game that night. My family thought it would be best to keep my mind off of everything.

However, it was an impossible task to even find the motivation to play. Overwhelming emotion, uncontrollable sadness, and fear of what the future held for my mom ate at me as I put on my uniform.

My first high school basketball game wasn't supposed to be like this. I always envisioned my family filling the stands having only one thing on their minds – a NewCath win. That was only a figment of my imagination now.

In reality, the outcome of the game didn't matter at all. I fought hard for my teammates, but it all seemed so pointless. All my energy was being used up to fight back the flood of emotion that crashed down on me at a moment's notice. Thinking about how my mom ended up with cancer was difficult to come to grips with. The sequence of events replayed in my head a million times...

A few weeks earlier (on Halloween 2001, to be exact), Mom had gone in for a scheduled mammogram, a common preventative approach for women over the age of 40. That particular time was filled with frequent trips to St. Elizabeth Medical Center because my Grandpa Krebs suffered from an apparent stroke and had been in the hospital for a few months because of troubled breathing and lung issues. Mom was busy trying to help my grandma deal with Grandpa being in the hospital, and with so much going on, she had forgotten to get her results.

I remember going with her to the hospital. We were slightly alarmed when we spoke with the technician in Radiology, who said they couldn't find her file. Even though it was odd, we didn't think much of it.

The following day, the Radiology office contacted my mom. They'd found the file and apologized again for the inconvenience. They encouraged her not to worry, but they also told her there were a few irregularities that needed to be checked. They recommended that she come back in for additional testing.

Questions had to surround her thoughts. What could they have found? What kind of irregularities? We weren't too worried because there was no history of breast cancer in our family, but it was only natural to feel a hint of anxiety.

On November 21, 2001, my mom had a biopsy performed to find out what was actually wrong. A few days later, on that glorious and picture-perfect Friday with clear blue skies, a nice cool breeze, and excitement in my heart about the first basketball game of my career, we got the news. My mom had cancer.

We didn't even know the whole story yet, but knowing it was cancer sent shock waves throughout my family. We were cancer illiterate. We knew nothing about bone scans, stage one, stage two, chemo, or metastasis. We were unaware at the time, but those terms would become all too familiar in the coming years.

• • •

We found out my mom's cancer was undetectable by a self-exam. The doctors found it only because of the mammogram she had done when she turned forty. The doctors couldn't explain exactly why the cancer occurred. Signs pointed to high estrogen levels and stress, but doctors are always slow to point out a direct source.

Once the family accepted the fact that it was cancer, we gave it our best attempt to be positive. Mom, along with the rest of the family, made the commitment to do everything necessary to be cured. That's when she met Dr. H, a physician with an impressive success rate with cancer patients, who recommended that my mom take a rather aggressive approach. The doctor labeled the cancer as Stage II and assured us that we could anticipate a cure with the right treatment.

A mastectomy – removing my mom's left breast – was the best option, and it was the next step on my mom's road to recovery. The surgery was set for December 21, 2001, the same night as my basketball game against Shelby Valley. Again, my family encouraged me to go to the game.

My mom implored, "Please go to your game. The whole family will be here to take care of me. By the time I get home from surgery, you'll be back from the game. Don't let your team down because of me."

Taking my mom's words to heart, I went to the game. During the entire four-hour bus ride down to the eastern part of Kentucky, my mind was back at home worrying about the surgery. It was wearing on me.

The game couldn't get started fast enough because I needed the thoughts to quit racing around in my head. As soon as the game tipped off, my adrenaline kicked in, putting me in the right frame of mind to play. That kind of thinking had worked ever since my mom found out she had cancer. There was no reason it wouldn't work again.

A back-and-forth game turned into one of the most exciting games of the season. We ended up winning at the buzzer on a last second shot.

On the bus ride home, I joined in the mayhem only after there was confirmation from my dad that the surgery went as planned. My worries were put to rest instantly. As a matter of fact, the surgery went so well that she was released from the hospital and was home only four hours after surgery was completed.

Of course, she had to deal with the surgical trauma to her body, the emotional impact of losing a part of her feminine anatomy, nausea and vomiting due to the anesthetic, and a Staph infection to top it all off, but we truly thought it was all worth it because this nightmare would soon be over. We hoped our worries would be put to rest. We believed the cancer would be gone.

We were sadly mistaken.

• • •

Christmas Eve of 2001 is a holiday that will remain imprinted in my memories forever. I recall how strange it was from prior years. Even though it was celebrated at my Aunt Joyce and Grandpa Seibert's house just like always, it was untraditionally solemn and quiet.

We awaited results from my mom's lab testing. It was the post-mastectomy test to see if the cancer had spread anywhere else. We eagerly anticipated the outcome. If her lymph nodes were cancer-free, there was an excellent chance that the surgery was a success, and my mom would be cured just like we had been praying for since her diagnosis.

Around 7 p.m. on the night before Christmas, with family filling every inch of the house, the phone rang. It was Dr. H.

Not a sound escaped a single person as we huddled around the telephone. You could have heard a pin drop. Mom sat silently listening as the doctor went through the results. Each of us focused intently, trying to interpret what was being said on the other end of the phone.

After only a minute of conversation, a single teardrop rolled from my mom's eye and onto her cheek. My stomach sank. Everything seemed to be moving in slow motion. An awful feeling began brewing inside. The news was not what we were hoping for.

Dr. H informed Mom that the cancer had been found in her lymph nodes. Ten of fourteen were showing cancer. It could have spread anywhere by now. There was a chance it wasn't just breast cancer anymore.

This news forced us to face our worst fears. The emotional challenge of trying to smile and be optimistic was fruitless. Trying not to cry was effortful. The word festive had been lost from our vocabularies.

I sat stone-faced trying to figure out why this was happening. Furthermore, why on Christmas? The time of year designated for giving and being jolly was now a holiday full of sorrow.

We felt sick at the thought of the cancer spreading throughout my mom's body. We felt even sicker when we found out that the first step of the mastectomy was not even required. We didn't realize Mom was supposed to have a bone scan performed right after the initial findings on her mammogram. Perhaps it was just an oversight, but even Dr. H was unaware that my mom didn't have one done. The surgical trauma to her body, the emotional impact of losing a part of her feminine anatomy, nausea and vomiting due to the anesthetic, and the Staph infection were all for nothing.

Sadness wasn't the only feeling that filled the house that Christmas; anger followed close behind. The news that the cancer was in her lymph nodes meant she was battling more than Stage II breast cancer.

It was greater than that, a bigger uphill battle for survival. Everything my mom had undergone so far was in vain.

• • •

Crying spread like an epidemic throughout the house. I gazed upon each and every face to see their grief and feel their anguish. I didn't know how to respond to the circumstances. Numbness was my only reaction. My heart hurt for my mom, and I wanted so badly to take on her burden. It was clear everyone in the house that Christmas wished for the same thing.

My parents didn't know it, but a small act of kindness was about to change the attitude of everyone. The phrase, "That's what family is for" never resonated quite like it did that night. Family was there to lighten the load any way possible for my mom.

I remember it vividly; Grandpa Seibert always gave each of us an envelope for Christmas that contained whatever he could afford to give us that year. Apparently, my aunts and uncles had had a secret meeting before we arrived. They all decided to present my mom and dad with their envelopes containing money to help with the initial financial costs of my mom's treatment. They thought the money could be used toward future bills and to help pay off the surgeries and tests Mom had already been put through. And there was no better time than now to brighten the mood.

As 9 p.m. rolled around, just as they planned, all the money was collected and offered to my parents. Andrew, who was 10 years old at the time, saw the gift the rest of the family gave to Mom and Dad.

Following their lead, he walked over to Mom, reached in his pocket, took out the $10 bill from the envelope he had received from Grandpa, and handed it to her saying, "Please take this money, I wanna help too."

With that warm-hearted gesture, a flow of tears from the eyes of everyone filled the room. Instead of crying out of sorrow, a sense of compassion overcame us. It was going to be an uphill battle, but we were all behind my mom to help her along the way.

• • •

We all knew my mom was going to need radiation and chemo-therapy to eradicate the disease. We were told numerous stories of how tough the road was going to be. Mentally, Mom pressed hard to get prepared to go down the path to remission. She created a plan to give her the best chance of surviving the brutal treatment.

Mom and Dad researched their options regarding treatment and doctors in the weeks following Christmas. They knew it was impor-tant to choose an oncologist quickly. The hunt was on.

Shortly after the new year, they visited Dr. B, a physician who came highly recommended and had the best success rate in the area. Immediately, Dr. B and Mom formed a unique doctor-patient relation-ship, and gaining confidence in a doctor was of extreme importance to her. She felt strongly that he was trustworthy and that following his advice was the direction she wanted to go.

Dr. B didn't know it then, but he was in for a treat, to say the least. After studying her charts carefully, he had the necessary information regarding the lymphatic system. He came to the conclusion that a bone scan should be the first thing done.

No one knew anything without a bone scan. It was uncertain if the cancer had spread from the lymph nodes to the bones. Dr. B stated that if breast cancer spreads, or metastasizes, it usually goes to either hard or soft tissue – bones or organs. He prefaced the tests by saying that if the cancer spreads, it normally doesn't attack both.

With that being said, the bone scan was performed. As a family, we kept our fingers crossed.

By the time the results reached my home, I was at a Xavier Uni-versity basketball game with my high school coach, Coach Detzel, and some of my teammates. A terrible snowstorm made the drive home nearly impossible, and it was rather late when I finally made it back. The sight of vehicles lining the street and driveway took my breath away. I silently gasped as the sickening feeling in my stomach once again hit me like a ton of bricks.

As soon as I entered the house, my dad guided me into the garage to explain what was going on. At this moment, an unusual feeling that life was never going to be the same overcame me. Dad tried his best to stay composed as he described the severity of the situation.

The news didn't seem possible. I didn't want to believe the cancer had spread to the bones. I couldn't bare to hear that tumors were present on her spine, ribs, and skull. The Stage II cancer was now Stage III.

After I processed the information as much as I could, I went into the house and gave my mom a hug. We didn't say any words, just embraced each other. It was an unpleasant reoccurrence, but a cloud of depression filled the house again. I wanted to cry, but I knew she needed comfort. Hope was not yet crushed because Stage III could still be treated.

• • •

It seemed that the basketball season was only a blur at this point. I had trouble concentrating and getting into the competitive spirit. The hunger for the taste of victory was gone. My family's world was shattering one bad result at a time. Unfortunately, more bad new was right around the corner. There was one more crushing blow to add to the others.

We didn't think things could get any worse until a few days later when Dr. B ordered an MRI Scan to check the soft tissue. Dad was picking me up from school at NewCath when I asked him if Mom had received her results. He tried his best to avoid the question. The answer was too much for him to put into words. Understanding his torment, I had a gut-wrenching feeling the test showed more terrible news.

My worries were well warranted; the MRI showed that cancer had also spread to the liver. Stage III was now Stage IV. In the blink of an eye, the cancer had become Stage IV, terminal, no remission possible. The time for life was limited, and the end was inevitable.

When we arrived home, the familiar scenario of my relatives' cars filling the driveway and street reinforced the awful news. Unstoppable panic set in. I felt helpless, as if time was moving too quickly to digest what was happening.

When would the chain of bad news end?

I opened the front door, glanced around the room at the sad faces I had grown accustomed to over the past month, and slowly retreated to my room upstairs. There I cried. With all my hope being crushed, weeping uncontrollably was the only thing I could do.

My Uncle Wayne followed me up the stairs to console me. I was so scared about how the family was going to cope. Life went from being stable to spinning out of control in a rapid whirlwind of emotion. The world, as I knew it, was crumbling fast, and there was no way to slow it down. The unknown was frightening, and imagining the pain my mom was feeling left me sick inside. I hated that she had to go through any of this.

How could I make it better for her? How do I make the sadness stop? Unfortunately, there were no answers, just questions.

My uncle, with hopes to calm the hurt inside, gently responded, "We are going to have to come together as a family. We are going to have to be here for one another. We are going to witness how strong your mom is. Let's have faith, and we'll get through this by being positive."

> **...the next few days, months, and years were going to be tough**

Knowing the situation had hit rock bottom, I gathered my emotions together. Quickly learning the value of composure, I knew it was time to be strong for the rest of the family. There was no doubt that the next few days, months, and years were going to be tough, but the only way to get through them was to roll with the punches and stay optimistic in the face of adversity.

• • •

At the next meeting with Dr. B, Mom built up the courage to ask a question that many would never want to know the answer to. She wanted to know what she was up against. She wanted to know how long she had left to live.

The answer hit her like a punch to the chest. He estimated that she had around 9 months to live, 18 months maximum. He said that how her body handled the treatments of chemotherapy and radiation were factors in how long she would last, but the biggest factor was her attitude toward it all.

Was life going to be worth fighting for?

Was seeing her kids each day worth the price of the pain and sickness this disease would cause?

Could her attitude withstand the face of death everyday?

She began to face these questions head on when she started her treatments of chemotherapy and radiation. Mom was loaded up on painkillers like OxyContin, Vicodin, and other high-powered medications to ease the sting of treatment.

The chemo was tough on her. At the conclusion of each visit to the hospital, she experienced vomiting, nausea, headaches, and fatigue. It drained her physically, mentally, and emotionally. It made waking up every day a chore.

The radiation was nearly unbearable, and it took its toll in a totally different form. The pain medications were necessary to combat the side effects of radiation, but they made her sit for hours staring into space. This scenario went on for weeks. I would ask her a question and there would be no response, just more staring.

We would all see the blank look on her face, and each of us thought, "This isn't right, this isn't living."

We would take turns trying to get her to eat, feeding her. We simply figured the treatments were too much for her to handle.

Weeks passed by and adapting to life without a coherent and conscious mother was difficult. It was sad, but as long as she wasn't in pain, I was going to give it my best shot to be in good spirits.

One morning, a pleasant surprise greeted me as I strolled over to the sink and tossed in the cereal bowl after finishing up my breakfast. The spoon and bowl made a loud clang as the glass crashed into the metal.

As soon as the bowl hit the sink, a familiar voice shouted at me from the hallway leading into the kitchen, "This isn't gonna cut it."

My heart jumped out of my chest. It was Mom.

She noticed that shoes and clothes were laying about, garbage in the can overflowing, dirty dishes sitting in the sink, pots and pans left on the stove after dinner the night before.

She proclaimed with a smile on her face, "Mom is back!"

I was never so happy to be scolded in my life. Andrew, Mandy, and even Dad felt the same. There was absolutely no resistance from anyone regarding the assigned housekeeping duties. We realized that Mom had taken herself off of most of the pain medications. She wanted to deal with the pain so that she could enjoy the life she had left. From that point forward, no matter how much pain the chemotherapy caused her, she dealt with it in a way that made life worth living.

• • •

It was a bitter truth, but the disease was changing all our lives. Mom was forced to give up babysitting, Dad was torn between going to doctor's appointments and teaching to make a living so the family could survive, and none of us seemed to leave the house unless it was for school or sports.

The economics of cancer loomed over us. Such a huge financial burden now added to the nastiness of the disease. With the ever-mounting medical bills, family and friends knew they could offer the most help by organizing a fundraiser.

Never wanting to be a charity case, Mom and Dad were both against it initially. My aunts and uncles pleaded with them and assured the two that this was something that needed to be done. Realizing they would do the same if another friend or family member was in their shoes, they agreed. Financially speaking, assistance was vital to continue the treatments. If there was any hope for a longer survival, aid was necessary.

Even though forming the committee, advertising the fundraiser, and organizing the entire event was new to all of us, it became larger than ever anticipated. The gymnasium at Newport Central Catholic was filled to capacity. Over a thousand people showed up to offer their support. Joy filled my heart to see the unconditional giving from friends and strangers alike. A long-awaited ray of happiness shined bright on my family during this night. At least for one evening, the horrors of cancer were put to rest.

As time passed, more acts of kindness followed. Friends held additional fundraisers, proceeds were donated from golf outings, and a barrage of food periodically found itself on our doorstep. Every single kind act made my mom's battle a little easier to fight.

By the 9-month mark, my mom wasn't even hinting at slowing down. Before we knew it, she was battling for over a year. Strength began building as soon as she combated the after-effects of radiation. As soon as she pushed through that, little by little the struggle started to loosen its grip on her.

Mom never reacted to the effects of chemotherapy like most cancer patients do. If she was supposed to lose her hair, she didn't. If she was supposed to have numbness in a certain area, she didn't. The typical reactions varied with her. Even though feeling sick was an everyday normality for her, she did not allow it to alter her lifestyle.

I'll never forget the first time she lost her hair. She had it shaved off because Dr. B warned her that the chemo would cause her to lose it one chunk at a time. This information hit her pretty hard. When she walked through the door in her brand new wig, we were surprised that it looked so much like her normal hair. After we all exchanged opinions on the hair, she shot each of us a mischievous look and without a delay, ripped the wig from her head. There she stood, bald. She asked if any of us wanted to rub her baldhead for luck.

Of course we did.

She laughed at herself, and we laughed at the fact that she was laughing. It had been a while since laughter filled our home.

Mom's motto quickly became "Live, Love, and Laugh" because it was the easiest way for her to see the light at the end of the tunnel. It was the best way to bring happiness to the gloom that could easily consume her life.

• • •

By now, I was in my sophomore year of high school. Mom no longer had radiation, and she was handling the harshness of chemotherapy like a champ. She bought into the idea that life, even at its worst moments, is worth living for.

Then in October of 2002, our faith was put to the test. We got some bad news, but this time, it didn't have to do with my mom. Instead, it was about Grandpa Seibert. He was diagnosed with pancreatic cancer and was informed that his body had been battling it for some time without his even knowing it. Just when we thought everything was under control in our lives, we were attacked on another front.

The doctors gave him days, maybe weeks. Grandpa looked around the room at all of us who were there to comfort him.

With tears in his eyes he said, "I didn't even get a running chance, not even a warning shot."

He only lasted two weeks. Each of us spent every bit of free time by his side. I will never forget watching his last moments on this earth. Even though he was fighting a losing battle, he found the strength and mustered up the courage to speak.

He looked up at my mom and said, "I will never give up because I don't want you to give up."

My mom grabbed his hand and said, "I know you are strong Dad. I promise to never give up. It's okay to let go. Grandma Marie is waiting on you in heaven, and I'll have everyone down here to help me keep fighting."

Not a minute later, with all his family in the room, he let go. On October 17, 2002, at the age of 74, Grandpa Irv, as he was affectionately called, was gone.

Needless to say it was another extremely emotional time for my family. It was yet another test to see how strong we were as a unit.

Mom continued fighting through the weekly chemotherapy treatments through my sophomore year and into my junior year. I fought hard in the classroom and on the basketball court, finding focus and resilience in the hard times I had to live through.

Doctor B continued to do everything possible to control the cancer in the soft and hard tissues. The number of tumors on my mom's spine reached above 100. Her bones were becoming brittle. She would lift up a laundry basket and break a rib. She had the mind of a 42-year-old but the bones of an 80-year-old. Doctors urged her not to lift a muscle; doing so could cause serious injury. The next day, she was moving furniture around the house as if everything were back to normal. Mom refused to live a certain way for the cancer. She was going to do things her way and not let the cancer dictate her life.

One thing is certain, she had character, and she continued to do it her way. At the 18-month mark, it was as if she were indestructible.

Dr. B learned quickly to never give her another deadline. He just kept the chemotherapy coming week after week, month after month.

• • •

Unfortunately, tragedy found us again in September of my junior year. Having been sick for a very long time, Grandpa Krebs passed away.

I was at school when a call to the office stopped me in my tracks. They explained that my grandfather had just died. Again, numbness was the only feeling that surrounded me.

It was a tough pill to swallow, but tragedies and bad news during high school were becoming routine. Just when things started looking up, tragedy seemed to strike again or the phone rang to present my family with more sickening news.

> It was easier to start worrying about other people

I remember just sitting at the funeral and staring. I found comfort in the memories Grandpa and I had shared. Remembering the kitchen basketball, trips to the park, and stories about the old days helped ease the pain.

I learned a valuable lesson about life while sitting at the funeral that day. It became apparent that wallowing in my own self-pity was very unproductive. I remembered the phrase, "God only gives you what you can handle," and I took it to heart. Through each of the horrible events in my life, I was building character, and even the tragic events happened for a reason. It was easier to start worrying about other people than it was to figure out why things were happening to me.

• • •

Unfortunately, my four years of high school didn't play out like I thought they would. Adversity seemed to lurk around every corner, and, at times, it was tough to find hope because my faith and that of my family was constantly shaken. Luckily, we had my mom's unyielding strength to rally behind.

She would use different occasions as milestones to reach in order to make it through the constant rounds of chemo. The 18-month deadline was long gone. Milestones like a birthday, a vacation, or a family picnic started turning into graduations, weddings, grandchildren, and events deeper in the future.

She even started to make chemotherapy like a day out with the girls. Cookies, brownies, and cake were taken to the hospital like it was a neighborhood bake sale. It may sound simple, but it played an essential role in getting her through the vicious cycle. Mom kept busy with hobbies like beading and making scarves. Perhaps her hobbies were the best therapy.

She would not allow us to dwell on the cancer. She wanted us to live normal lives and knew there was no point in her fighting if it meant holding the rest of her family back. Life wasn't worth living if it meant heartache and misery for those around her. She wanted us to move forward and live each moment for a brighter future.

A little over a year into treatment, Dr. B told my Mom something that changed her life forever.

He said, "I know a person doesn't have long to live when they begin living for the cancer. They give up their daily life for the disease. That's when they eventually give up and lose."

Mom refused to let that happen to her. She wanted control of her life. Realizing that her secret to survival was not giving into the cancer, she was not going to let setbacks take her control away. She knew that her attitude was the most critical part of survival, and she was right.

> ...her attitude was the most critical part of survival

# 4

# COURAGE
## Realizing Priorities

Throughout high school, basketball became the biggest outlet for me. It was a release from the stress and worries at home. It allowed me to get away and escape for short periods of time. I always felt it was an effective way for me to cope with the situation of my mother's cancer and its impact on my family. Plus, sports were something my whole family could share in together to help us deal with our daily dose of adversity.

I would work out all summer and would spend every day shooting baskets in the gym by myself, sometimes with my dad, and many times with my little cousins who would come along and rebound for me. Shooting relaxed me, and it was a skill I constantly wanted to improve. Being able to shoot the ball at a high percentage was a way to always be valuable to a team.

My high school days at NewCath were consumed by sports of all kinds. After dabbling in football and baseball early on, I eventually decided to center my focus on golf and basketball.

During my junior year, I actually qualified for an individual spot in the state golf tournament. I shot my best round of the season at the regional level to receive an individual berth to state. That was honestly one of the high points for me during high school sports. It was an unexpected gem, so to speak.

I played baseball for only one year, but it was fun stepping back into it after a couple of years off and playing on the same team as some of my childhood friends. It seemed useless for me to take baseball too seriously, though, because I thought basketball was the best way for me to get a free education in college.

Being well aware of my family's situation and the strain a disease like cancer can be on finances, I set a goal to get my college education paid for. No one told me I had to get a scholarship if I wanted to go to college, but I knew it would be one less thing for my parents to fret over. So, with this goal in mind, I set out to spend all my time and energy on the sport I loved most, basketball.

As it turned out, my four years of high school basketball were a success, and I had a very productive career, despite the fact that I was so thin that my uncles and Dad actually gave me the nickname "Skinny." They also called me "No butt" and would ask if I lost my butt in a poker game. All I could do was laugh because they were right; I measured in at a whopping 6' 4" and only 160 pounds. Being so thin, most of the other players I competed against overpowered me. Regardless, I fought through my slight build and relied on shooting and skill to outperform the others.

My skills and abilities on the court progressed nicely throughout high school. In my senior year alone, there were about eight games where I scored over 30 points and had a career high of 47. I was a member of the "1,000 point club" and received a multitude of all-star and player-of-the-year awards.

More important than individual achievements was the success my team had during my four years. It wasn't because we overpowered our competitors' athleticism but because every player on our team truly loved the game. We understood the value of preparedness.

Throughout high school, I learned the importance of a confident yet humble attitude. We felt like we could win every game but knew we had to outhustle the opponent to do so. In essence, high school was where I learned the key to winning: The will to win is more powerful than athleticism and skill. My team was a small example of that.

• • •

My high school preparation helped me land on AAU and all-star teams during the summer months, and with them, I got to travel all over the U.S. and even over to Europe. Basketball allowed me to visit different places in the world, and it was a big part of my growing up.

The first trip away from my family was over to Milan, Italy to play against other international teams. I stayed there for a little over a week the summer before my senior year. We had the opportunity to split up in twos and stay with an Italian family. Getting to play against international competition and living with a family with a mother, father, son, and daughter was a once in a lifetime experience. Being there taught me the value of communication. Asking for food and drink was a chore, but the most difficult task was being away from my home, my family. I loved Italy, and even though I had the yearning to get back home, I found myself enjoying every sight and sound. The experience was eye opening, to say the least.

In addition to Italy, I also traveled to Houston, New Orleans, and Orlando among other places. Basketball offered me the chance to see the world for the first time in my life. Seeing the level of play throughout the world was invaluable because it reminded me how far I had to go and how hard I still had to work.

However, my most memorable moment of high school didn't happen on the basketball court or another playing field. It didn't come in the form of a packed house on a Friday night or from the chants and cheers of a rivalry game. It wasn't in the inspiring words of Coach Detzel nor did it require leaving the country. I didn't need a uniform of any sort to experience the one thing I will always remember from high school.

# I came across a letter from my mom

All it required was an empty room on my senior retreat. At NewCath, senior retreat was a chance for the seniors to get away for a few days. We were able to reflect on situations at home. We were given the opportunity to assess our place on this earth and were encouraged to open up to peers to find answers to critical questions. At the retreat, I found out what people actually thought about me. In doing so, I found out a lot about myself. I'll never forget sitting alone one night on that retreat, reflecting on my life. As I rooted through letters that my family and friends had written to me, I came across a letter from my mom. The letter pulled at my every emotion. It read:

*Dear Marky,*

*I hope this letter finds you doing well at your retreat. I pray that you have discovered a lot about yourself over the past couple of days. I want you to know how truly strong you are. Life hasn't been easy for us the last three years. I promise to continue to fight for you kids because I never want to leave you. Your dad and I are so proud of you and all you have accomplished so far. It's amazing how fast you have grown up. I can remember like it was yesterday when you were born and having kidney surgeries. I loved the fact that you would always search the room to find me. You always knew I was with you. I am not sure if I will ever get to see you walk down the aisle with your beautiful bride or if I will ever get to see you become a father because I don't know what God has planned for me. You have made an awesome son and brother to Andrew and Mandy so I have no doubts that you will make an excellent husband and dad. You hold all the confidence in the world in your eyes and I know you will be successful. Remember to always live, love, and laugh because look at me, life is too short and living is a precious gift.*

*Love,*
*Mom*

Tears flooded my eyes as I struggled through every sentence. Until that moment, thoughts of my mom's illness beyond the present never existed. I never pictured my wedding day without her there. I never imagined my son or daughter without a Grandma Terri. I wept uncontrollably. I envisioned all the milestones of my future and they all seemed fruitless, tainted. It was easy to understand my mom was battling cancer, but I never actually saw her losing. Life without my mom was unimaginable until this letter put things into perspective.

The retreat, along with all that I learned there, helped prepare me for college and the recruiting process. As a child, I wrote out a list of important goals I wanted to reach. One goal in particular was to play on a Division I team that played on television. Dreams of playing in front of thousands of people bedazzled me. But by the time high school hit, I was pretty levelheaded and realized a school like the University of Kentucky was unattainable. Therefore, after narrowing my aim to smaller Division I programs that were prominent colleges where I could earn my degree and prepare for a successful career, I knew basketball could aid in my ambitions. It could open doors to help me achieve my wildest dreams.

My first recruiting letter came during my sophomore year from American University, a very prestigious Division I program, and I was excited at the prospect of getting more contact from other schools over the next few years. Getting that first letter and being wanted by other colleges and universities was incredible.

But just like the rest of my high school career, my mind raced out of control during the recruiting process. If you ask any player who has gone through it, I think you'd find that the whole process can become quite burdensome. You take a massive number of schools and break them down, pros and cons. Opinions come in from all your friends and family on what they think would be the best fit for you. Thinking of my mom weighed into the decision-making process, as well. With so much going on, I started to become burned out and lost interest in the sport I once loved.

Basketball seemed to matter less and less as my mom's cancer progressed. Basketball was only a game; my mom's situation was life and death. Family came first. Moving far from home for college was out of the question, and graduation was closing in. I hadn't picked a college, yet, and I couldn't come close to making a decision because my family's battle preyed on my mind constantly. Basketball became the last thing on my mind, and the least of my concerns.

• • •

High school typically represents the glory years, but with my mom being sick, the focus on graduation, and my future college prospects, it was difficult to see it that way. It all seemed impossible to deal with at times, but there are some memories that made everything worthwhile.

Perhaps one of my most special moments from high school was being able to go to the "Mom Prom" at the end of my senior year. My mom felt well enough, or at least said she did, to be my date for the dance.

Thinking back on everything she'd been through, I knew the dance was a special time for both of us. We ate dinner together, shared some laughs, and more importantly, danced the night away. Mom was an amazing date. As a matter of fact, we won the twist contest.

As we danced, I couldn't help but think about the hundreds of tumors that covered her bones. I couldn't imagine the pain she felt but continued to fight through in order to make memories she and I would never forget.

After we won the twist contest and the judges held up our hands as the champions, my mom leaned over to me and whispered, "You know they just let us win because they felt sorry for me because I'm sick."

I shook off her assumption and replied, "Absolutely not, Mom, we won fair and square. We were the best."

Not only was I fortunate that she was healthy enough to attend, but also that she had the strength to enjoy herself. We shared a special night that will remain etched in the forefront of my memories forever.

• • •

A few weeks later, as graduation approached, my mom was admitted into the hospital. She was very sick. As usual, she was being hampered by a massive number of tumors on her spine, but she also had an infection in her lungs. My mom's immune system was so badly depleted that the pneumonia could have devastating effects.

My preparation for graduation was overshadowed by constant trips to the hospital to visit her. Everyone feared the worst for my mom, and the doctors prepared us as best they could. We thought it might be the end of the road.

Mandy stepped in to attend the array of ceremonies leading up to the night of graduation. My dad and Mandy were going to be there for me in person, but I knew my mom was going to be there in spirit.

I remember the afternoon of my graduation. Sitting on the side of my mom's hospital bed, I could see the tears beginning to form in her eyes. It was a milestone for her to see my graduation. It was one of the things on her bucket list that got her through the weekly horrors of chemo and the never-ending sickness. It crushed her spirits not to have the strength to see me walk across the stage to receive my diploma. Understanding her chances of being at the ceremony were slim, I struggled to stay positive.

Anticipation began to set in for the commencement ceremony. It was amazing to reflect back on all that had transpired over my four years. It was incredible how much life had changed and how fast I was forced to grow up. However, my heart ached to think about my mom lying in her hospital bed, possibly nearing the end of her fight.

While standing in line with the rest of my class, getting ready to make our big entrance, I looked around the room at my classmates in their caps and gowns. I thought about the music, the speeches, the diplomas, and about leaving high school and heading to college. When we began marching into the gymnasium, thoughts of my mom laying miserably in the hospital ate at me. I needed her there.

As I approached the stage in front of the gym where we would all take our seats, I peered off to the left to see my dad, Mandy, and Andrew sitting just to the side of the stage. All of my aunts, uncles, and cousins joined them. Then, to my surprise, seated on the floor in front of them, I saw my mom, sitting in a wheel chair with a mask over her face. The entire family was gathered around her.

Apparently, my mom begged the doctor to let her go and told him she would like his permission, but even without it, she was leaving the hospital. Reluctantly, Dr. B and the hospital staff agreed to it. He knew my mom, and when she said she was leaving, she meant it.

He arranged for the wheel chair, provided her a mask to wear, and made her promise to return by midnight, just like Cinderella. The mask was one of the stipulations of her being able to leave the hospital so she didn't catch any germs.

## ...it was an unexplainable thrill

None of that mattered to me, though. I grinned from ear to ear simply because she was there. She made the journey for me and wasn't going to let any obstacle keep her away.

When I looked up and saw my mom, it was an unexplainable thrill. What courage, what a show of love for family. Even though the mask covered her mouth, I knew she was smiling. Her eyes were full of pride, and so was my heart.

• • •

After the conclusion of graduation, I had to make my final decision on where to attend college. I lined up my priorities; Mom was at the top of the list. Being there with family had to be my first priority.

While she was battling for her life in the hospital, sports needed to take a back seat. Staying close to home took on a new importance.

With that in mind, I decided to attend Thomas More College, a nearby Division III school. Not only would I receive a large amount of financial aid thanks to my grades in high school, but it was a fantastic academic institution. In my mind, an academic scholarship was better than an athletic scholarship because I wasn't sure how much longer my athletic career would last anyway.

Because Thomas More was my dad's alma mater and only ten minutes from my home and because I was able to continue playing sports there, it became my final decision. I was eager to play basketball and golf at the college level. With my family's full support behind my decision, I was ready for the transition.

# 5

# DESIRE
## Chasing the Dream

My choice to go to Thomas More College after high school seemed like a great decision. After my mother's near-death encounter, it was necessary to be close to home, close to her. Even though she made it to my graduation, the intense pain was almost too much for her to bear. She had huge tumors covering the surface of her spine, pneumonia plagued her lungs, and her immune system was so compromised that the doctor warned us to be prepared for whatever might come next. So we braced for the worst.

If you asked any of my family members if we thought she'd make it through that episode, the answer would have been no. I believed it would take a miracle, but the likelihood was slim to none.

To my amazement, one day, a few weeks after graduation, her body began to get stronger. It fought off the pneumonia and infection, while radiation decreased the size of the masses on her spine to something more manageable. The hospital became a little easier to visit because each day my mom recovered more and more.

Her survival only reinforced my college decision. I understood that at any time my mom's health could take a turn for the worst. It would have been absurd to move across the country just to play basketball. My family needed me, and I needed them.

Nevertheless, for now, Mom was back to her old self. Life was back to semi-normalcy, and I was eager to begin college.

My situation aside, Thomas More was a great place to make the transition from high school to college. It offered me the chance to play basketball and participate in golf, and most importantly, the opportunity to stay close to home, but it was also a great school with a challenging curriculum. The people there were unbelievably generous, kind, thoughtful, and down-right good people. I made many friends there and felt comfortable in the environment. Thomas More College was the best fit for me at that time in my life.

• • •

In the fall of my freshman year at Thomas More, I sat exhausted on the couch at my house watching the University of Kentucky's Big Blue Madness. As I was an avid Kentucky fan, the event never ceased to amaze me. I was in awe at the 23,000 fans that showed up at the opening practice of the season.

One by one the players ran out of the tunnel and onto the floor to a standing ovation. The crowd cheered as the team was introduced. It was chaos. I envisioned myself being there, and for a second, my mind began to wonder.

I thought about myself standing in the tunnel, dressed from head to toe in my Kentucky uniform, listening as the announcer started my introduction, "From Newport, Kentucky, 6'5" shooting guard, Mark Krebs."

A thunderous roar followed as I trotted to center court. I thought to myself, how cool would that be?

Watching Big Blue Madness got me thinking about my first season at Thomas More. Although it would be nothing like playing at the University of Kentucky, I couldn't wait for the season to kick off.

• • •

Hard work during the preseason and early regular season practices prepared me for what to expect. Although I was only a freshman, I truly believed there was a legitimate chance of me being a starter. Without question, I knew I could contribute greatly to the team's success right away, despite the fact that we had 25 players on the roster at the start of the season.

In my opinion, that was way too many players. Our basketball coach was also the Athletic Director at Thomas More. He handled his duties terrifically, but it had to be challenging for him to wear so many different hats. He gave us all the time he could, but I always felt he had so many other things on his mind and too many other things to do.

It also surprised me that our workouts leading up to the season weren't as difficult as I thought they'd be for a college-level program. Figuring that my 6'5" and 170-pound frame would be put through a body-altering experience, I envisioned forming big muscles after spending many long hours in the weight room.

When I first arrived at Thomas More, my pencil-thin arms and bony chest couldn't even bench press 100 pounds. Sometimes I'd even mistake the outline of my ribcage for abs. I was definitely afraid I'd be easily overpowered in the weight room by my teammates and that I'd have some serious catching up to do. Shockingly, that wasn't the case.

Being extremely weak for a college athlete, I was willing and ready to do the work necessary to improve. All I needed was some direction on how to get it done. It was impossible to see how the weight and conditioning program was going to prepare me for the season because it lacked a great deal of physicality and guidance.

Nonetheless, I was confident that the year was going to be a success. I brushed off my worries as nerves that stemmed from the thought of competing at a new level.

• • •

The first game of my college career rolled around rather quickly. We lost on a last-second shot in overtime. It was a heartbreaking game, but I finished with 27 points, not a bad opening game if I do say so myself. The second game couldn't have come fast enough. I knew what to expect and felt exceedingly confident after my first performance.

However, severe disappointment set in when our coach stayed true to the platoon system. With 25 players, Coach tried to play everyone by substituting five players at a time, every four minutes. With so many guys and the substitution of five at a time, it was nearly halftime when it was finally my turn to check back into the game. The platoon style disheartened me and sucked the competition out of the sport. It removed any hunger to win that I had inside of me. After scoring 27 points, I imagined I'd get more playing time, but that was far from reality.

As a result, my enthusiasm began to drop as the season advanced with each game and practice. The enjoyment I usually found in the sport was lost. I started to question whether or not I really wanted to suit up anymore. The thought of going on road trips made me ill. My drive to succeed was gone, and the thrill and excitement were gone with it. I basically sleepwalked into the next few games. For weeks, it felt like my mind and body were pulling separate ways.

In addition, only a scarce crowd came to the games to cheer us on, and because of the rotation, it was difficult to get into any rhythm when I actually did get to play. At least in high school, there was a gym full of fans that could ignite my interest even when I was on the bench. A crowd is a sure way to get the blood pumping, but unfortunately, Thomas More didn't have one.

Honestly, the lone reason I continued to play was because my family would travel to watch the games. My quitting would disappoint them because I'd never quit anything in my life. But with my mindset and the feelings in my heart, playing for Thomas More was impossible. I was only hurting the team if I kept playing.

After taking everything in my life into consideration, I had to ask myself, "Why should I keep playing if basketball wasn't going to be fun anymore?"

No matter how hard I tried, it just wasn't in me to do my best. I had to make a change.

. . .

On a cold and crisp winter morning, December 23, 2005, to be exact, it was odd making the drive to Thomas More, not for practice and not for a game, but to have a talk with Coach. The things I had to say couldn't wait until after the holiday season.

Standing outside Coach's office door, I tried to gather my thoughts before entering. Like always, Coach greeted me with a warm welcome as soon as I entered the room. We discussed my feelings toward basketball. I explained to him that I wasn't taking this decision lightly and that I'd been searching for some type of answer for weeks. Sadly, there was no other option except for me to step away from the game.

Quitting hit me hard. Not only was it difficult for me to deal with quitting something for the first time, but the realization that my basketball career was really over stirred up more emotion than I ever imagined. It ended so much faster and earlier than I'd ever planned.

I thought back to when I was a kid and about all the basketball I'd played up to this point. Did I really practice countless hours for it to end like this? The answer made me sick, but my mind was on too many things, especially my mother's health. I still loved Thomas More, but I was confident that quitting was the right decision. Luckily, I still had golf and wouldn't have to pay for school; it was a huge relief that my scholarship didn't depend on athletics.

. . .

Even without basketball, I made it a point to stay focused on my priorities, making sure they were in line.

Since practices and games no longer tied up my time, I was able to spend almost all my time during the next few weeks of winter break with my mom and family. Those were a crucial two weeks for me to enjoy moments with family. I was able to clear my mind

## Supporting her was important to me

and take a deep breath for the first time in a long time. It also afforded me the opportunity to take my mom to chemo treatments and doctor visits. It was something that I was sheltered from while in high school and didn't have time for in college. Obviously, these weren't ideal circumstances, but being there for my mom through the pain and suffering of chemo was something I needed to do. Supporting her was important to me.

She already knew it, but I wanted to show her that I would be by her side through anything. So one day we made a trip to the St. Elizabeth Medical Center for a weekly round of chemotherapy together.

I'll never forget what it felt like to walk through the automatic sliding doors of the Oncology Center for the first time. As we made our way down the chilly hallways, it was remarkable how warm I felt next to my mom. She brought her usual brownies and cookies for the nurses and was greeted with open arms by every single person. She lit up every room we entered.

After the routine preparation, the nurses seated her comfortably in a chair. I looked around at the patients sitting comfortably in their respective recliners with IV's standing at their sides. People of all ages, shapes, and sizes filled the room. It would've been such a cold place if my mom had given up hope. It was plain to see how people could get depressed going to a place like this. Instead of giving into the doom and gloom around her, my mom made it feel like we were at a get-together with her friends. She and the rest of the patients shared laughs all afternoon long. It was truly an impressive sight to see.

Throughout the afternoon, I was handling things pretty well until they began pricking at her port with a syringe. The port, which was located in my mom's chest, was an easy way for the nurses to hook someone up to IV's over and over again. It kept a vein constantly ready to accept the drip of chemo into her body.

I wanted to pass out because the sight of needles made me queasy, but it remained my objective to stay strong. My mom didn't like needles either, but she had grown accustomed to them over the years. It saddened me that her life support was a slow drip of poison into her veins. I hated knowing that sickness would weaken her for days and that by the time she felt good again, it would be time for another round. It was such a vicious cycle, and until that day, I couldn't fully appreciate what she went through on a daily basis in order to spend precious moments with her family.

Going to chemo that day changed me.

• • •

Before I knew it, it was a week into the new year of 2006. Spending time with family over the Christmas holiday made the time fly by.

While I awaited the start of my second semester, I woke up one morning in a bit of a panic. It dawned on me how much I truly missed basketball. The emotions hit me all at once, and I had the sudden urge to play again. I wanted to be part of a team full of dedicated players. I wanted to feel the excitement of winning. I longed for a team where things mattered and people wanted to be the best they possibly could at the sport. In essence, I wanted something more than Thomas More could offer me.

UK's Big Blue Madness that I saw on television a few months earlier popped into my mind. Seeing the dedication painted on the faces of the fans made an impression on me. I recalled the players and how proud they were to be representing UK. The feeling and drive to be at Kentucky was strong within me. No matter where I went or what I did, the desire to be a Kentucky Wildcat consumed me.

After deciding not to tell anyone about my aspirations, I planned out the course of actions I'd take to make my dreams a reality in secret.

For starters, I began working out religiously. Growing tired of being skinny and weak, I wanted to develop my body. No longer was I going to sit around and wait for the right strength program to come along and change me. It became clear that being proactive was the only way to accomplish anything. I needed to focus on not only getting my body stronger but also strengthening my mind. It was important for me to believe I could achieve my goal.

Doing some research on the topic, I looked at UK's roster and knew they would be losing Ravi Moss and Preston LeMaster as walk-ons the next year. The timing seemed impeccable. However, the next step was tricky.

How could I get in touch with Coach Tubby Smith? He seemed like an amazing person, and something inside me told me he'd probably hear me out if I could just talk to him.

I soon decided to write him a letter about my interest in playing for UK. I looked up the Kentucky Basketball contact information on-line, and in my letter, I explained that I was committed to working hard and trying out for his team as a walk-on. I included my grades from my first semester at Thomas More and a list of my achievements. It seemed like a shot in the dark, but it was worth a try.

After sealing the envelope and dropping it in the mailbox, a strange sense of hopefulness came over me. I was eager for his response.

In the meantime, I tried to keep up my grades at Thomas More and prepared for the spring golf season. All the while, I kept my dreams secret; I didn't want to share them with anyone until I knew for sure they were within reach. Putting my head down and moving forward, I went back to work.

• • •

Almost two weeks had passed, and I had heard nothing.

Finally, my mom called me on the way home from class. She informed me that I had a piece of mail from Kentucky Basketball. I nearly wrecked the car I was driving in excitement. Impressed by the quick response, I still wasn't sure who'd actually written the letter. I also didn't know what it said.

Nerves and speculation took over until I picked up the letter for myself, opened it, and read the words that Coach Smith himself had written.

It said simply, "You would be a great candidate as a walk-on. My staff and I will keep you in mind."

What did that mean? Did I need to contact him again? Was he going to contact me? I was ecstatic, but there were so many new questions swirling around in my brain.

It was time to finally explain to my family what I'd been plotting. Mixed emotions filled the room. My dad didn't want to see me fail, and everyone else thought it was a great idea in theory but believed it was a little far-fetched. My family was happy to see me excited, but they remained apprehensive. None of that bothered me, though.

The things I was planning to do seemed like a pipe dream to most, but one calculation that everyone failed to see was how unbelievably driven I was to succeed. It was going to take a lot to deter me from reaching my goal. I used everyone's doubts to fuel my desire. My hard work all these years and this letter told me that I could reach my destination. I remained positive that Coach Smith was offering me a chance to make it.

With new motivation, I went back to work, trying my best to gain weight and bulk up. People were amazed at the progression I made physically; my skinny frame was filling out and growing stronger every day. I finished my first year at Thomas More with a 3.91 GPA, 20 pounds of muscle, and a hunger to achieve the goals I set out for myself.

• • •

Because I wasn't technically playing a sport and because I wasn't sure about UK yet, I had to get a summer job. It was my mom's rule.

The best decision I made was taking a job working with my Uncle Joe. The company that hired me was responsible for putting up residential and commercial swing sets and basketball hoops. It was the perfect summer job, and, more importantly, my uncle and I got to be together.

He understood my dream and suggested that we should both head to the gym and work out together at five o'clock each morning. He knew that workdays were long and finding time to work out at night would be tough. So we made a pact to get physically and mentally stronger together. He knew I wanted more than summer work and college, and he appreciated that I wanted to push myself to higher limits.

As the summer went by, the anticipation became intense. What was my next step? Did the letter really mean something? Was Coach Smith just telling me what I wanted to hear and secretly hoping I'd go away so he wouldn't have to hear from me again?

I quickly realized that kind of thinking had to end because it wouldn't get me anywhere. Of course, it wasn't conventional to go from a Division III school to play at the Division I level, let alone at the University of Kentucky, but for some odd reason, it felt like fate. I needed to believe in the desire that was driving me toward Kentucky.

> **Could you stand looking back in 20 years knowing you didn't even try to reach your dream?**

Even though I stayed optimistic, no one else really believed Kentucky Basketball would have a spot for me. Most people couldn't accept the fact that I was even entertaining the idea, but then again, they didn't have the faith in me that I had. As a matter of fact, my Uncle Joe was the first person who really encouraged me.

On the way home from work one day I remember him saying, "Could you stand looking back in 20 years knowing you didn't even try to reach your dream? Could you live with the fact that you'll never know what might have been? Remember, you only live once and can never get those dreams back."

Those were powerful words for me to hear, and his support and encouragement were special to me.

Lying in bed that night, I thought about what life would be like if I actually went down to UK. Could I really leave my mom when she needed family the most? She was fighting so hard to live and experience things with her family. Could I bear to spend so much time away from her? Before going any further, I needed to talk to her.

• • •

The next day, I found an opening at lunch to discuss the prospect of leaving home to pursue my dream.

She responded to my worries by saying, "We have a strong family, and UK is only a little over an hour away. Go for it; take the risk. I will always be with you, and we will make the trip down there as much as we need to. Time and distance won't be anything we can't handle."

It was all I needed to hear. Her words moved me into overdrive. At this point, I had worked my way up to a solid 192 pounds – 30 pounds more than I was 3 months earlier. I was in the best condition of my life.

Understanding that my dad was cautious and didn't want to see me fail, I was certain he would come around as soon as he realized how strong my determination was. But for the time being, I had the blessing of my mom, and that was all I needed.

Soon after receiving my acceptance letter to the University of Kentucky, I signed up for the orientation for incoming students. Before making the trip to Lexington, I'd put together something that had to come with me. It seemed important that Coach Smith receive the packet I'd worked on for nearly three weeks straight.

Contained within the packet was my personal campaign to get to Kentucky. I prepared a resume of all my accomplishments, my stats, my grades, and a player profile. I also explained my workout schedule for every single day at 5 a.m. I placed all that into a binder, along with letters of recommendation from well-known individuals throughout the state who knew me on a personal level.

As soon as I stepped foot on campus, I wanted to make sure everything I'd put together ended up in the hands of Coach Smith. We drove directly to Memorial Coliseum and made a stop at the basketball office.

The tradition of Kentucky Basketball hit me instantly. A tingly feeling filled my stomach as I opened the door to the basketball office that overlooked the historic Memorial Coliseum playing floor. After walking up to the receptionist, I asked if I could hand deliver my binder to Coach Smith. She apologized and informed me that he was out of town recruiting. But she assured me that she'd personally deliver them to his desk right away, and I trusted her.

• • •

The next few weeks left me calling and calling, persistently annoying the UK Athletic Department because I wanted to make sure Coach Smith had received my information. The waiting game had to end. I received a little more information with each phone call, and it wasn't long before I was talking directly to Coach's secretary. She put my worries to rest when she confirmed that he'd read everything of mine.

That news excited me considering it had been months since the vague letter from Coach. I needed something more to sustain my motivation.

Within a few days, I finally received the letter I'd been waiting for.

It was another letter from Coach Smith, and it read, " Mark, I love your work ethic and grades. Everything I have reviewed looks great.

I promise you nothing except that you will get an opportunity. Please stay in touch."

This letter was all I needed to keep the fire alive. Even though there was a risk that basketball might not work out at UK, I was ready to give it a go. I'd given too much blood and sweat and too many tears to back down now; Coach Smith was willing to offer me a chance. That's all I could ask for.

• • •

While eating lunch one day near the end of summer, I received my first phone call from an assistant coach at UK. He asked me to report to the basketball offices at the start of the fall semester in August. When the call ended, my heart thumped with excitement. Words could not describe the joy I felt that day.

There was no doubt about it; I was prepared to prove to everyone that I could play at a Division I program. Even though what the future held for me was a mystery, I was on the verge of something special. I had the blessing of my mom, who was as strong as she had been since her diagnosis. Her strength encouraged and inspired me. I was ready to take my basketball career, my academic pursuits, and my dreams to the University of Kentucky.

# 6

# MOTIVATION
## Never Give Up – A Lesson from Mom

It was a beautiful day in August, not a cloud in the sky. Stepping foot on the University of Kentucky campus as an actual student was thrilling. I felt the excitement of the students around me, especially the freshmen, who were moving away from home for the first time in their lives. The emotional sensation that came over me was unlike anything I'd ever experienced before.

Small twinges of homesickness ate at me as I began to think of things I'd be without, but it was exhilarating to know I would be on my own. The training wheels were off. No one was there watching and questioning my every move. I was going to miss being home, sleeping in my own bed, and eating lunch with my mom every day, but I had a mission to accomplish. Even though I was nervous about making the team, I kept a positive outlook. Being eager to get started was an understatement.

• • •

Thankfully, my family came along to lend a hand with the move-in. They helped me adjust to my new life in Lexington, and all of them were instrumental in calming my nerves.

The dorm I was assigned to happened to be none other than the legendary Haggin Hall. My life away from home was to begin in one of the oldest dorms on campus. I suppose that's what I get for my late enrollment. My uncle said he stayed at Haggin in the 1960s when he went to UK. From the look of the place, it hadn't changed much.

Despite its age, Haggin was actually conveniently positioned at the center of campus next to the library, where I would be spending much of my time. It seemed to be near all my classes, and, more importantly, it was only a 15-minute walk to Memorial Coliseum, where I hoped to soon practice basketball as a new member of the Kentucky Wildcats.

As my family helped me carry my toiletries, bedding, and clothing up the four flights of stairs to my room, I surveyed the layout of the building. It was set up in a complete square with a courtyard open in the center. Sidewalks jutted off in each direction to hallways A, B, C, and D. It reminded me of a scene from a prison movie, and I was heading to cellblock 4D.

As my dad, mom, Andrew, Mandy, and Aunt Joyce walked me up to my room on the fourth floor, we weren't sure what to expect. It was an old building and leaned heavily on the depressing side. As I put my key in the lock, turned the handle, and pushed open the door, I felt overwhelmingly suffocated. The room couldn't have been more than 12 feet by 12 feet.

There was a set of bunk beds on the left with a wooden desk connected on the end. The two pieces of furniture covered the entire left wall. On the opposite side of the room was my roommate's desk, along with a single armoire that the two of us would share. In addition to this furniture, a heating and air conditioning unit covered the far wall.

I immediately wondered where my TV would go. I looked around at all of my belongings and came to the conclusion I would have to do without most of them. These were tight quarters that I would have to share with someone I had yet to meet.

It was a shame that I already hated being away from home, was sad to be leaving my family, and felt uneasy about the random roommate.

Although I had to fight hard to quiet the feelings of homesickness, my enthusiasm remained high about the opportunity to play basketball. But I couldn't keep my mind from racing as I questioned my survival in these conditions. I kept telling myself that it wouldn't be long before I moved into the Wildcat Lodge with all the other basketball players. I assured myself that everything at this stage was just temporary.

· · ·

After putting the finishing touches on my room and saying good-bye to Mom, Dad, and the rest of my family, I couldn't help but wonder how crazy I was to give up a scholarship at Thomas More only to take out a $15,000 loan to attend UK. Fearing that I might be making some sort of mistake, thoughts cluttered my mind and nausea filled my stomach.

It was natural to have second thoughts, but fortunately, I never lost sight of my purpose. Knowing with all my heart that what I was working toward was special, I was able to push aside the negative concerns, feelings, and thoughts and concentrate on more optimistic views. I was going to make my dream happen even with the cost of tuition and my uncomfortable living conditions. I had been offered an opportunity to compete at an elite program, and I wasn't going to let a few minor inconveniences stop me from fully embracing that opportunity.

Just like always, I turned to my favorite coping mechanism during troubling times. I relied on working out and shooting baskets to help me get through my bouts of homesickness and spurts of second-guessing myself.

The exercise center at Kentucky was incredible, and state-of-the-art equipment was at my disposal. A running track, countless treadmills, weights, and four basketball courts were all there for students like me to use, and I had three days until classes would begin. That was plenty of time to get acquainted with my environment and to begin preparing for the challenges that lie ahead.

At the top of my agenda was introducing myself to my random roommate, catching up with old friends, and maintaining my focus – because the next day was my meeting in the basketball office.

• • •

After a long night of tossing and turning in bed, thinking about my upcoming meeting, I was ready to start my journey across campus. I vividly remember the sights and sounds of the walk to the basketball office at Memorial Coliseum. Beautifully stamped walkways, tree-lined paths, and time-honored buildings were only a fraction of the scenery.

There was a unique kind of energy and a strange feeling of freedom as I approached the front doors of the basketball office. As I pulled open the giant glass doors, I was cordially greeted by one of the ladies working at the desk. After I explained to her that I was Mark Krebs and was scheduled to meet one of the assistant coaches as instructed by Coach Smith, a puzzled look appeared on her face as she checked the schedule sitting in front of her. She began rudely whispering back and forth with a coworker.

She turned to me and apologized by saying, "I'm sorry, but there's no record here that you're supposed to meet with someone."

I was speechless for a second but eventually began giving them details of the prior events leading up to this encounter. Both of them rolled their eyes at me in disbelief. I could see their doubt going to work. Who is this guy? Mark Krebs who? How can we let him speak to an assistant coach when we know nothing about him? They continued to look at me as if I was certainly in the wrong place.

Feelings of insecurity quickly turned to frustration. The women did a great job of making me feel unwelcome, but somehow, their behavior only assured me that I was in the right place. Even though the ladies made me feel incredibly uncomfortable by talking to each other as if I weren't there, I kept my composure. I knew the truth and kept reminding myself that Coach Smith wanted me there. Every sign pointed at leaving, but I waited patiently instead.

Finally, after about 15 minutes, an assistant coach walked through the door. I promptly explained my situation and told him my entire story. Thankfully, he knew exactly who I was, and we spent the next few minutes discussing my basketball career, work ethic, and what I had been doing up to that point.

After hearing me out and promising that Coach Smith would follow through on his offer of an opportunity, he said, "I will certainly tell coach you came by the office. Since the guys have been out of town for a couple of weeks, they'll be eager to play some pickup games tonight. Be here around 7:00 pm. It'll give you a chance to see how you compete."

I couldn't believe my ears. I was surprised I was going to begin playing so soon. When the conversation ended, I picked up my backpack, smiled to the ladies behind the front desk, and headed back toward Haggin Hall.

• • •

All day long I kept trying to picture in my mind how the night would turn out. The anxiety was wearing me out.

When 6:00 p.m. rolled around, I began my 15-minute jaunt across campus to the Coliseum. I was nervous, to say the least, and I got more and more butterflies in my stomach with every step. But at the same time, realizing what I was about to do made me feel like I was walking on air.

I stood in front of the Coliseum with my NewCath duffle bag around my shoulder, a grey cutoff t-shirt, black shorts, and all the confidence in the world.

Once I arrived, it was clear that I had jumped the gun. Looking at my phone, it dawned on me that I was 45 minutes early. Each door I tried to open was locked. It wouldn't have been surprising if a security guard had tried to stop me for breaking into Memorial Coliseum.

Finally, around the side of the building I found a door that hadn't been latched shut. I pulled it open and found myself in a dark hallway.

Walking softly and slowly, I weaved in and out of hallways trying to find my way to the gym.

Suddenly, the faint sound of a bouncing basketball grew louder and louder. Cautiously, I stuck my head around the corner to see who was on the court. There was one person on the far end shooting free throws. To my surprise, it was Rajon Rondo. The Boston Celtics had just drafted him after he played two years for Kentucky. I didn't realize at the time that he would end up as one of the premier guards in the NBA and a World Champion, but I was still in awe to see him. After walking over to the bench and sitting in admiration for a minute or two, I proceeded to lace up my blue Nikes.

I eventually built up the courage to walk over to Rajon. I introduced myself and told him why I was there. Then the two of us shook hands. As we shot around, I explained to him my journey to Kentucky and how I planned to be a walk-on. He was extremely friendly and receptive. He continued to explain what I was up against and educated me on Coach Smith, informing me about his style, his demeanor, and his expectations. It was information that I believed was necessary for my success. I nearly went scavenging through my duffle bag for a pen and notepad to write it all down.

After about a half hour of shooting and talking back and forth with Rajon, the entire team came out of the locker room and started filing out onto the court. They had their white dry fit shirts, blue shorts, and team shoes. I aspired to be one of them, but in the meantime, I felt totally out of place with my grey cut off t-shirt and black shorts. I kept reminding myself to be patient. If I proved myself as a player, I'd be able to work my way into a uniform and shoes. At the moment, though, those things were the least of my worries because I still had a long way to go to earn a spot on the team.

It was comical when I started introducing myself to the players. I went around the gym from player to player, talking to veterans on the team like Joe Crawford, Ramel Bradley, and Randolph Morris. I tried to play it cool by asking them their names, but like any hard-core UK fan, I already knew them all! It was impossible not to know each of them from all the games I'd watched in earlier years. Trying to introduce myself to the team in a nonchalant manner was useless because inside I was like a kid on Christmas morning. I already knew all their statistics and hometowns, majors, heights, weights, and years in school.

In the state of Kentucky, there were no major professional sports teams of any kind, so Kentucky basketball was basically a "religion" and fans really believed they bled blue. As soon as UK players sign on to the team, they instantly become heroes. Autograph seekers and photographers follow them wherever they go in the state.

Needless to say, I knew the players on the team well and wanted to be one of them. That's what my dream was all about, playing for the University of Kentucky in front of 23,000 people at every game. Being part of such a great basketball tradition would be the pinnacle of my athletic achievements.

• • •

After I struggled through my introductions with the players, it was time to play some basketball. Before the first pickup game, Rajon chose me to be on his team. To be honest, I couldn't have asked for anyone better than him to teach me the ropes. Not only did he tell me what I needed to do but he also showed me how to do it. He gave me hints on how to earn respect from the guys, and he encouraged me to be confident because I belonged at Kentucky.

Throughout the night, he talked to me about the practices and explained what it would take to make the team. He alleviated many of my worries. With each new game, I performed better and better, knocking down a few three-pointers and driving to the basket for a lay-up on occasion. Defensively, I held strong despite the fact that I was outsized by every player on the court. I was pleased overall, and after that first night, I remember changing my shoes and sitting on the sidelines with the team feeling like I belonged.

Excitement carried me back to the dorm that night. I was worn out and my body ached as I headed to Haggin Hall, but a strange euphoria overcame me. As soon as I stepped foot outside of Memorial Coliseum, I called my mom and dad to tell them how well it went, explaining in detail every encounter, every play of the game. They relayed the message to the rest of the family, but I was still on the phone the entire 15-minute walk and well into the night because each family member wanted to hear everything first-hand.

After I concluded the last phone call and the adrenalin and enthusiasm died down, I called my mom back. This was the beginning of my calls to her every night before going to bed. She wanted to know how my day went, and I wanted to know how she was feeling.

From my perspective, talking to her every day and night helped me get through everything that confronted me at UK, and I believe she looked forward to the calls, too, because they let her know I was ok. Sometimes all we exchanged was an "I love you" and a "good night," but it still meant the world to both of us.

## ...it still meant the world to both of us

My mom had been through a great deal since her diagnosis, but at this particular point, she was feeling great. Luckily, her body was responding well to the chemo treatments, even though she'd had over 250 of them in her five years of fighting.

To look at her, you'd never know she had cancer, and it was impossible to tell she had been through an astronomical amount of chemo. Giving up was never in her vocabulary. She was full of energy again, loving life and seemingly gaining strength each day, and that helped make being away a little easier for me to handle.

• • •

I played pickup games with the team a few more times before classes officially began. And being so excited about basketball, I forgot to check out the campus to see where all my classes were located.

On that first day, there was no doubt about it; I was lost. I walked out of the dorm, clutched my schedule in my hand, and walked aimlessly to find my first building. Since I'd stepped foot on campus, I had only needed to know one direction, one building, and one road: the one to Memorial Coliseum. I had no clue where my classes were going to take place.

I noticed a steady flow of students was walking along the library in the direction of the north side of campus. After merging into the stream, I began asking people for assistance. The first student I approached asked me to walk with him because he was headed to the same building. Unfortunately, I had to follow the same routine with each class on my schedule. I wandered around the campus like a tourist in New York City for the first time. All I could do was laugh at myself.

After a long first day of classes in buildings all over campus, I returned to the dorm exhausted. I wasn't lying in my bed relaxed for five minutes when suddenly the phone rang.

Surprisingly, it was the basketball office calling to ask me if I could report to the office as soon as possible because Coach Smith wanted to meet me. I didn't walk this time; I ran across the campus with a little added pep in my step. Upon entering the office, I was invited back to Coach Smith's office. It was there that I met him for the first time. Just as I suspected, he was a very pleasant man.

He shook my hand and said, "I am glad to finally meet you, Mark. I was happy you contacted me about your interest in trying out for the team. I hope everything has been working out for you. We will be

## I was still in a position to make my dreams a reality

starting conditioning and individual workouts as a team in the next few weeks. I will have one of the assistant coaches call you to stay in touch. They will let you know when you need to be here."

As the conversation ended and we exchanged our good byes, I felt confident about my chances. Even though nothing was set in stone, Coach gave me the motivation I needed. I was still in position to make my dreams a reality, and that was the best part of it all.

# 7

# PERSEVERANCE
## Thanks to Tubby, A Wildcat at Last

Over a month had passed since my discussion with Coach Smith. It was already early October, and I was still only playing pickup games with the team. I was playing well, but I didn't know how to feel since I hadn't even had a true workout yet. My patience was wearing thin, and uneasiness was setting in.

Nonetheless, staying in shape remained my first priority so I'd be ready when the opportunity presented itself. My classes got better as I adjusted to the new environment, and I stayed sharp physically by putting myself through my own basketball drills at the student exercise facility.

My goals at the time totaled three: first, doing well academically; second, remaining at the top of my game athletically; third, staying out of trouble. To stay motivated, I concentrated on how much I would eventually help the team instead of why I didn't belong. I was positive I had done everything right to earn my opportunity.

My worrying was put to rest when I received a call from the basketball office informing me that I needed to show up for the team practice the next morning.

The assistant coach spoke enthusiastically, "We want to see what you can do on the court with the team. Hopefully, you've stayed in shape over the past month. Coach wants to see how you can contribute. Based on what we've been hearing about the pickup games, we believe you've earned your chance. Be at the Coliseum at 7:45 a.m. for workouts. They'll have gear for you over in your locker at that time. Get a good night's rest, and we'll see you tomorrow."

After the conversation ended, I sat up silently in my bed. I couldn't stop smiling! How could I possibly go to sleep after a phone call like that? My mind raced, palms grew sweaty, and heart beat rapidly as I lay there thinking about the upcoming practice. I couldn't help but replay the assistant coach's words over and over in my head. Sleep was impossible. The familiar feelings of anxiety and excitement that I'd had as a child before a big game found me again. I reminded myself to take deep breaths because getting a good night's rest was crucial.

Just like every night, the last thing left to do was call my mom. As soon as she answered, I started explaining the conversation I'd just had with the assistant coach, and, like always, talking to my mom really helped calm me down. By the time I got off the phone with her, my body was relaxed and ready for bed.

• • •

October 10, 2006, was not only my twentieth birthday but also my first day of practice with Kentucky Basketball. I awoke with unbelievable energy, got dressed, and started my hike across campus.

The skies were overcast as I approached Memorial Coliseum, and as I arrived, I saw the entire team stroll out of the building and into a set of blue vans that were parked on the street. I immediately grew concerned. I pulled my phone from my pocket and glanced at the time. It was only 7:30 a.m. There's no way I was late. Running to the nearest van, I anxiously grabbed one of the team managers.

"Where are you headed?" I asked in panic.

He responded, slightly agitated, "The team is heading to the indoor football field to run. Everyone was told to be here early. Vans leave at 7:30. You're a little late don't you think?"

I couldn't believe what I was hearing. Coach never once informed me about the change of plans. In only a few moments, I went from being fifteen minutes early to being late.

The manager apologized, "I don't know what to tell you, man. I'll get in trouble if we aren't over there as soon as possible."

In a panic, I ran inside the Coliseum to Mr. Keightley's room (he was the equipment manager at UK for nearly 50 years) and pleaded to him to give me my gear because the team was about to take off.

He raised his voice at me, "Why are you so late? You can't do that on your first day. Don't you know better than that?"

I was taken aback by his shouting. It scared me that he seemed so disappointed. I actually couldn't believe the legendary Mr. Keightley was scolding me. There was no time to explain the misunderstanding about the time. All I could do was offer my deepest apologies for the mistake.

He finally gave in, "Hurry and get your gear from your locker. You're the second one on the left. You still might be able to catch one of the vans."

I sprinted to the locker room as quickly as possible, unsure if I should be happy to have a locker or nervous because I was so late. There was no time to think about it. I needed to hurry.

I found my locker and threw on my brand new practice gear and shoes. Sadly, I didn't even have time to enjoy all my new attire. This morning was turning out to be a nightmare.

Weaving through the hallways, I realized there was no way the vans had waited for me. My heart sank as I pushed the door open and confirmed my fear. The vans were gone. Just when I thought the day, my birthday nonetheless, couldn't get any worse, it started to rain.

I stood alone outside the Coliseum in the rain, uncertain of what to do. Missing my first workout with the team was out of the question.

Even though the coaches might excuse my lateness, I knew it was important that I make an effort to be on time.

After taking a second to assess my dilemma, I realized my only option was to run across campus toward the football stadium. The indoor facility was about as far as you could get from Memorial Coliseum and still be on campus. It was over a mile run, but I knew I had to make it.

Rain rolled down my face and drenched my clothes, but it didn't discourage me. I drudged along with wet socks and waterlogged shoes all the way to the practice facility. By the grace of God, I managed to get there just as the team was beginning to stretch, so I quickly filtered into the exercise lines. I was a tad bit wet but otherwise unscathed. In fact, the dart across campus was a fantastic warm-up. I was ready to begin my first workout as a Wildcat.

• • •

The setting at the indoor football field is one I'll never forget. It was awe-inspiring to be among the players I'd watched for years on television.

I stood in the exercise line trying to imagine what it must feel like to run out on the court at Rupp Arena, what it must feel like to have so much pressure resting on your shoulders. Living up to the remarkable history of Kentucky Basketball couldn't be an easy task.

I wondered where they found all their confidence? How did these guys find the courage to perform at such a high level?

I found the answers to those questions rather quickly.

To push myself through the conditioning, I had to dig down deep. It was the toughest thing I had ever been through up to that point. We sprinted laps around the track, performed agility drills, and ran line touches on the football field. Pushing through each and every running drill, I fought hard to never give up – even when my legs and lungs burned uncontrollably. I trusted in my body to make it through. Picturing the word "Kentucky" across my chest and "Krebs" printed across my back, I told myself that the sting I was experiencing was nothing but sweet pain.

I quickly figured out the confidence the players exhibited came from unbelievable preparation and hard work. If I gave everything I had on a daily basis, I would be infused with poise and self-assurance too. This life-change was one I was looking forward to experiencing.

• • •

After I finished the workout and went through a long day of classes, my mom and dad called to let me know they were on their way down to Lexington for dinner. Because I wanted a big steak dinner for my birthday, they decided to take me to a steakhouse downtown.

As we entered the restaurant, the hostess escorted us to the back dining room. Shockingly, my whole family, including aunts, uncles, and cousins, were there to shout "Surprise!" as I walked in the room. They told me it wasn't just a birthday gathering but also a celebration of my first practice with the team.

After explaining to everyone how the conditioning went, I informed my family about the rules of being a transfer. Even if I officially made the team, I would have to sit this season out. I'd still have to practice everyday, but I wouldn't be able to dress for the games until next season.

> **I need to survive to see you put on that uniform**

I'll never forget the way I felt when my mom leaned over, gave me a big hug, and whispered, "That's no big deal. You gave me something to live for next year. I need to survive to see you put on that uniform."

At that point, I realized making the team wasn't a personal goal anymore. It was something my family needed in their life, a reason to fight through the difficult times. I was ready to endure the trials necessary to officially get on the team.

• • •

I didn't have to wait long before I pushed my body to its maximum and put my endurance to the test. Typically, each practice I attended and every workout I completed became a little easier than the one before it, but that was about to change.

Out of the blue one day, I was informed that I had to participate in an individual lifting session with our strength and conditioning coach, Scott Hollsopple, so that he could assess my strength. I was confident I could overcome anything he challenged me with.

I was in for a rude awakening, to say the least.

The number of repetitions I had to do of pull-ups, push-ups, and leg presses were nearly ridiculous. I knew my body was testing its limits when a strong feeling of nausea overwhelmed me. My arms, legs, and neck were nearly immobile.

Soon after completing the last few sit-ups of the workout, I wobbled into the bathroom of our locker room. I knelt down beside the toilet and instantly threw up everything that was once in my stomach. I had heard of people vomiting from running too much but from lifting? That was a new one for me.

> ## I had to make perseverance my number one task

Looking back on it, this was my "welcome to the team, kid" kind of moment. It was my initiation, so to speak, and each test I endured was another step toward becoming an official member of the team. At this point, I had passed all the tests that had been put before me. I knew that if I wanted this journey to continue, I had to make perseverance my number one task.

• • •

It was amazing to see how far I had come. Big Blue Madness of 2006 marked the end of a spectacular year for me. I thought back to everything I had been through since watching last year's event from my couch in Newport. I was now sitting in the stands at Rupp Arena watching my teammates being introduced. It was no longer just Kentucky Basketball anymore. Even though I represented a "red-shirt" walk-on position, the lowest of the low on the athletic hierarchy, I was still excited about participating in all the practices, working out with the team, and finally being where I wanted to be.

Who cares if I had to red-shirt?

To be honest, I was blessed to make it this far and wasn't planning to stop now. Dressing and being on the bench as an active player was in store for me next season; I just had to wait.

So as my family and I sat enjoying Big Blue Madness, I was filled with the motivation needed to keep pushing toward making my dreams come true.

• • •

The opening of basketball season brought a lot of excitement along with it, and not all of it happened on the court. One exciting occasion in particular had nothing to do with sports at all.

On October 28, 2006, Mandy and her longtime boyfriend, Neal Hester, tied the knot. It was amazing to see hundreds of family members and friends there to celebrate the beautiful day. The autumn wedding was extra special because my mom was there to see her daughter get married.

Just four years earlier, this had seemed impossible. No one ever thought my mom would be around to experience so many milestones with her children. However, slowly but surely, she checked one item at a time off her bucket list. After constantly setting goals to live for, she was finally starting to reach some of them. The wedding was another milestone for my mom. She had already marked off seeing my high school graduation and her 25th wedding anniversary. Up next were Andrew's graduation and the welcoming of her first grandchild into the family. It's incredible how the more her list grew, the stronger her will to survive became.

My mom's determination guided me into the regular season. It may sound funny, but the first bit of UK Basketball I had ever seen at Rupp Arena was that year's Big Blue Madness. Because of my own healthy schedule of basketball games, I had only watched the team on television up to this point. I attended a UK game only one other time in my life, when they used to play one game a year in Cincinnati, but I had never seen a Kentucky game at Rupp.

At the beginning of the season, Coach Smith approached me at the conclusion of one of our practices.

He said, "Even though you can't be in uniform, I still want you to sit on the bench during the games. Dress in a shirt and tie. You won't be able to travel, but you'll be with us at every home game. You'll have a spot on the bench."

It meant the world to me to hear him say that. When I walked in the locker room at Rupp Arena for the first time and saw the white home uniforms hanging neatly from every locker, it dawned on me that I was only one step away from wearing one of those jerseys. It was going to be a difficult task to wait my turn, but I had to have patience.

Looking forward to the season ahead helped me get through the anticipation of wanting to play in the games. In addition, starting out particularly well also helped. We beat rivals Indiana and Louisville early in our non-conference schedule. Just as Coach Smith promised, I sat in my suit and tie at the end of the bench during every home game. I was in every huddle, team practice, workout, and meeting.

If you had asked me when it was that I actually made the team, stepping foot on the court for the first time would have come to mind. Uniform or shirt and tie, it didn't matter to me. When I walked out from the locker room with the team, stood through warm-ups, and cheered from tip-off to the final buzzer on the same bench as the Kentucky Wildcats, I knew I had made it.

• • •

Even though I definitely felt a sense of belonging on the team, I never actually heard the words, "You have made the team, Mark." However, there was one moment, aside from sitting on the bench during games, that put my mind at ease.

As we entered into the season, I struggled with not living on north campus or anywhere near Memorial Coliseum. It wasn't the fact that I was the only member of the team not living in Wildcat Lodge that bothered me because I certainly understood the circumstances. I was aware that by the time I began practicing with the team, it was already halfway through the first semester. It was only natural to feel a little like an outcast, but the physical distance from the team didn't bother me.

It was honestly the fear of oversleeping for practice that got to me. I had to set three alarms to calm my nerves. I figured one or two might fail, but three alarm clocks failing in the same night was unlikely. I even went as far as to use some that were battery-powered so that even if the electricity happened to go out, I would still be at 8 a.m. practice the next morning. Maybe being late for my first practice with the team affected me a little too much, but I couldn't afford to let a slipup like oversleeping ruin my standing on the team.

Obviously the trip back and forth to Memorial Coliseum was taxing. Making the 15-minute walk each way three times a day took a rather large chunk of my time, but I never complained. It took a lot of effort, but I knew my place. I was lucky to be there and proud of the hard work I had put in to make it happen.

Then one day, the team academic advisor, Mike Stone, asked how I was able to make it to all my classes, practices, and lifting sessions on time when I lived in a dorm in the center of campus. I intentionally made sure my current living situation didn't sound like a burden, but, as we talked, it became clear to him that it was an everyday challenge.

The next day Mike Stone spoke with Coach Smith about my situation. He told him that it would be best if I could move into a dorm across from the practice facility for the second semester. Coach Smith understood the situation and went to work fixing the problem. I was living in a dorm on north campus by the start of the new year, and I knew right away that life was going to be much simpler. It meant a lot to me that Coach cared so much about my personal well-being and situation. To me, it was reassurance that he wanted me to be a part of the team.

• • •

Things were coming together by the time Christmas break and the start of the second semester rolled around. It was such an exciting time for me, especially getting to celebrate New Year's Eve at Coach Smith's house. He invited us all to his home so we could celebrate as a team and family.

When we walked up to the porch in the front of the house, he was there to greet us in a cooking apron. He let us know that he was going to be doing all the cooking for us. On the menu were red beans and rice, steak, chicken, and all the side dishes you could imagine. After dinner, we spent the night playing pool in the basement and enjoying his home entertainment center as a team.

The conclusion of the party brought with it a new year, and the new year brought the completion of the Joe Craft Center. The multi-million-dollar basketball facility was truly state-of-the-art. Extending off the back of Memorial Coliseum, the Joe Craft Center provided new practice courts for both men and women, as well as locker rooms and exercise facilities that included training and weight rooms. The three-story addition created new administrative and coach's offices, as well. It was one of the best team facilities in the country.

In only my first year at Kentucky, I was already experiencing a number of exciting changes. Amazingly, I had no idea what was in store for the rest of my career.

• • •

Despite so much excitement surrounding a great start and the building of the Joe Craft Center, frustration plagued the rest of the season. Sure, we won many of the games we were supposed to win, but we lost far too many in the last minutes. As a team, we went an entire season without one surprising victory, and forget the idea of pulling off an upset because that was out of the question.

Throughout the frustrating season, I looked to my mom for inspiration. I needed her patience to stay in the moment and her strength to deal with the shameful loss we suffered at the SEC Tournament, along with the resulting 8-seed we received in the NCAA Tournament. It was going to be an extremely long road to the Final Four, but I had faith we could do it.

After beating Villanova in the first round, we lost in the second round to a powerful Kansas team. A season's end is always miserable, but this particular time, it also meant my red-shirt year was complete. For me, it was the silver lining on the rain cloud because I knew the next season was my time to shine.

• • •

A week after the season ended, Coach Smith had a meeting with each player to discuss where he stood for the next year. I was excited to meet with him because I was eager to see what role he wanted me to play on the team.

When I entered his office, Coach Smith greeted me with a warm welcome like always. Then he told me he saw me as being a part of next season's team.

He said, "Barring any unforeseen circumstances, I see you back on this team next season. You can help us in practice, and, if you work hard, I see you earning some minutes."

He went on to tell me the usual: Keep your grades up, stay out of trouble, and work hard during the off-season. After a few minutes of conversation, Coach Smith started opening up a little to me. He began revealing what basketball really meant to him.

I will never forget what he said to me during that one-on-one meeting, "Mark, I truly love basketball. I could sit in this office for 24 straight hours studying film and learning about the game. My wife wouldn't be too happy, but I could do it. Basketball isn't a job, it's my life and passion, and I love it. I enjoy seeing the young men I coach succeed."

It was nice hearing his encouraging words and listening to him speak from the heart. Coach Smith had a unique way of making you feel at home when he talked to you. I liked that.

I was excited that Coach Smith wanted me around the next season, and I felt relaxed knowing my fate was set for the following year.

• • •

Sadly, in an instant, that relaxation disappeared completely.

The week after my meeting with Coach Smith, I received a text message alerting me about a team meeting in the locker room. I wasn't too worried and figured it was to discuss what we needed to do to close out the spring semester.

All of us players sat around, casually sharing jokes and laughs, trying to get to the source of why the meeting had been called. Within moments, the assistant coaches, along with Coach Smith, began filing into the room. Coach after coach walked in with the look of despair on his face. Even Coach Smith walked in with an unusually solemn expression.

He began speaking with an uncommonly soft voice, "I want you all to know that I love each and every one of you guys."

I could tell by the tone of his voice that he was about to reveal something awful.

He continued, "There are times in life when you have to make a decision and times when you have to choose what is best for your family. Ten years at any program is a long time, and I feel blessed with the time I have had here. I am honored to have been able to coach at the University of Kentucky."

I could see the tears forming in his eyes.

I knew the words that were coming next, "I wanted you guys to hear everything from me. I will be going up to Minnesota to talk with their administration. I want you to know that you guys will always be special to me and my family. I want to thank all of you for the hard work and dedication you gave me on the court. It is never easy to say goodbye, and you guys can still come to me for anything."

Then the coaches exited the room just like they entered, sad. I didn't know what to feel. I didn't know what to think. My dreams instantly turned to dust.

Was I really losing the coach that had given me all these opportunities? Would I still be part of the team next year? Once more, I was left with only questions and no answers. Again, I felt lost and shattered.

# 8

# DETERMINATION
## The Gillispie Era Begins

It took a few days to come to grips with the fact that Coach Smith was leaving Kentucky Basketball. I struggled to stay hopeful and doubted I would be asked to play on the team when the new regime arrived. Being a red-shirt walk-on the previous season, I figured the new coach would come in and politely ask me to move on with my life.

People around the campus strongly anticipated the announcement of the new coach, but I didn't care too much. Fearing I wouldn't be back on the team nagged at me. The news stations were doing their best to narrow down the candidates for the general public, but it was tough for me to listen. I kept hearing through the grapevine that Billy Donovan from Florida and Rick Barnes from Texas were leading the race.

As the process dragged on, Randolph Morris, one of our potential senior leaders, decided to leave early for the NBA rather than finish his senior season. Each change brought more anxiety. I wondered if my basketball career would end when Coach Smith left for Minnesota. With so many unanswered questions stirring in my head, my dreams were quickly turning into nightmares.

I found myself tossing and turning most nights, but that didn't last. After only a few weeks of wandering aimlessly without a coach,

I finally awoke one morning to the beep of a text message. As I rubbed my eyes and looked over at my alarm clock to see that it was only 7 a.m., I wondered who could be texting me so early.

I flipped open my phone to read, "Meeting in the lodge to welcome the new head coach at the University of Kentucky, Billy Gillispie."

I recalled reading about how Coach Gillispie had turned the program around at Texas A&M. He was probably one of the best up-and-coming coaches in the NCAA. No doubt he seemed like a good coach, but his reputation of leading brutally difficult practices already preceded him.

As I made my trip across the parking lot to the Wildcat Lodge, I worried about just how demanding Coach Gillispie might be, but then I realized how little any of that mattered. All I wanted was another chance to prove myself worthy of playing the sport I loved.

We weren't waiting but five minutes when Coach Gillispie walked into the room. He entered, dressed nicely in a suit and tie, and introduced himself to each and every one of us. After exchanging a little chitchat with some of the returning players, Coach started off the conversation with some harsh observations and assumptions. He made it clear that, as a team, we were not a single unit.

In fact, I remember him saying, "Look how you all are sitting. Your chairs face in all different directions."

"He doesn't waste any time," I thought to myself.

He continued, "You will all be different in a few weeks. We will be together. All your chairs will face the same direction because we have one common goal – to win."

I guess he wasn't being completely negative, just honest. He concluded his first meeting with us by offering how truly excited he was to be our coach. After we all shook hands and said good-bye, he headed over to Memorial Coliseum so the fans could welcome him to Lexington before his scheduled press conference.

• • •

When all the press conferences, interviews, and obligations were over, it was time for the first workout with Coach G at the helm. After we had gone "coachless" for two weeks, his one-hour practice was the most difficult I had ever been through. I remember trying to dribble the ball but being so worn out that I could barely stay conscious. I was in a dizzy exhaustion, and my head was in a fog.

How could he expect me to perform well on the court when I couldn't even catch my breath? Not to mention, Coach G never sugarcoated anything. He informed us that we were the most out-of-shape team he had ever been around and that he was there to change our attitudes through tough workouts and practices.

I was proud to have made it through that first practice and knew I would be stronger the next time I stepped on the court. I did, however, feel for Joe Crawford and Ramel Bradley. Being the lone seniors, Coach G focused mostly on their actions. We could already tell their senior seasons were going to be difficult journeys, to say the least.

As a player, it was difficult to accept the changes because each passing day meant new faces throughout Kentucky Basketball. New assistant coaches, new staff support, a new strength coach, and a new trainer were all hired while very few people from the old system remained. It would take time to adjust to all the changes because the faces of Kentucky Basketball were virtually unrecognizable. Seeing so many people leave the program, I was amazed that Coach G kept me around through the spring. I continued to take one day at a time heading into May.

• • •

The month of May gave me more time with my family and gave the team the addition of more recruits. Among the recruits was McDonald's All-American, Patrick Patterson, and boy were we excited to have him on the team. He filled a very necessary void in the program, especially with Randolph Morris's leaving.

Upon my return back to Lexington for summer conditioning, Coach Gillispie called a meeting for the returning players. I was pleased to have been called and informed about the meeting because it meant, at least for the moment, I was back for another season.

The assembly of the new Kentucky Wildcats was filled with apprehension, and sickness overcame my stomach as I listened to Coach G elaborate on what he expected from us during the off-season. The only real thing the meeting accomplished was scaring the living daylights out of me.

Coach discussed the details of our daily agenda and explained what the summer workouts would entail. He also introduced us to the concept of "boot camp."

He explained, "The fall workouts I like to have are very difficult and focus on team unity. You better take the summer workouts seriously because you will be pushed to the limit each and every day once boot camp rolls around. When you hit your limit, you can't stop, or we'll just have to start over the next day at 6 a.m. My team isn't going to be a bunch of soft babies. We have to work like we're playing our first game of the season now."

I left the meeting overwhelmed. Coach G was tremendously intense, and it was going to take some time to get used to. I just kept reminding myself that it was all going to be worth it in the end.

## As always, I found inspiration in my mom

However, I tried to add the number of sprints we would have to do in my head, and it was such a large number I couldn't do it. I imagined boot camp as physical and mental torture. How bad did I really want to wear this uniform? How much did I really want to play?

In order to succeed, I would have to make determination my number-one attribute. As always, I found inspiration in my mom, and I planned to use that inspiration to push myself to the limit. I thought about all of the pain, discomfort, and sickness my mom had endured for nearly six years. It eased my worries about my own situation. I realized that what I faced was nothing compared to her daily struggle. Thinking about the strength of my mom made me stronger.

> I needed to keep pushing forward to achieve more

I also thought about my dad and all the time he took to teach me everything I needed to know about basketball. I owed it to both of my parents to keep fighting. To shy away from a physical and mental challenge was out of the question. I was too close to stop now. The pinnacle of my dream was not just a shirt and tie on the end of the bench. I needed to keep pushing forward to achieve more.

• • •

Just as Coach G promised, intense conditioning and an infinite number of sprints consumed the rest of summer. It was especially important for me to give each and every workout my all. I had to lay everything out on the line if I wanted to remain a part of the team. Thankfully, until the end of summer at the very least, I was still there.

When the fall semester arrived, I made it a point to meet with Coach Gillispie. It was imperative to see where I stood. Even though I was uneasy at the notion of talking one-on-one with the new coach, the meeting with him confirmed that I would be given the opportunity to play on the team. Coach told me that he liked having a large team and respected walk-ons. He assured me that I would be given the same consideration as all the scholarship players, and every guy on the team would get a fair shot at playing time.

"If you earn it, you get it," he insisted.

After a long and grueling summer, I was excited about being back in Lexington for the start of classes, and after meeting with Coach G, I was even more excited about the beginning of the new basketball season. And living in Wildcat Lodge with the rest of the team was a pretty pleasant perk of its own.

I could already envision my uniform hanging neatly in my locker at Rupp Arena. Images of the team plane set to take off for an away game played in my mind. Now that I had decided to keep pursuing my dream, and Coach G was keeping that door open for me, I focused my attention on the intense conditioning that lay ahead.

• • •

I vividly remember the night before boot camp was set to begin. Sleeping was impossible as I kept thinking about the dreaded drills, practice, and running that would take place at six o'clock he next morning. Boot camp was going to be four days a week for two weeks and would consist of full days of workouts that would only give us free time to eat, sleep, and go to class. Three workouts a day seemed cruel. There would be conditioning at 6 a.m., practice after classes in the afternoon, and lifting after practice. Not to mention the two hours of mandatory study hall from 7 to 9 p.m. There would be times my body would breakdown, but I knew it was important for me to keep fighting.

The next morning I awoke with a sick feeling in my stomach. The nauseous feeling only grew worse the closer I got to the practice facility. But I found comfort in the fact that I would be going through everything with my teammates; I wouldn't be alone. Just like Coach said over the summer, we all needed to rely on one another.

When we all stepped foot on the court that morning, ready to endure the torture of boot camp, none of us had to say anything. As we looked around the room, we all knew we'd have to help each other out.

My hope for that morning session was that every player would show up with a great attitude, Coach would take notice, and we would survive the first workout unharmed. As you can imagine, it didn't go quite like that. Instead, we did 30 straight minutes of defensive slides up and down the court without a break. Our first drill became the only drill of the morning.

Each time I thought we had completed the slides correctly, Coach G would stand there with his arms crossed and a smirk on his face, and he would say something like, "Perry didn't go as hard as he could go. Let's go again."

After five minutes, I wanted to cry. Every muscle in my body burned uncontrollably. By the 30-minute mark, death seemed eminent. Exhaustion had set in and catching my breath was out of the question. Every ounce of my energy had been spent. Each player was on the verge of crumbling.

Finally, out of disgust, Coach blew his whistle to end the workout.

He shouted, "Just get out of here. No one in here wants to go hard. Show up this afternoon with better effort."

It is sad to admit, but I was kind of happy. If we'd had to do another conditioning exercise, the trainer may have had to pick me up off the court. My knees were almost too wobbly to stand, much less to slide up and down the court. It was truly a blessing that Coach ended the workout when he did, and even though it didn't go as planned, the team made it through the first morning of boot camp.

• • •

When our afternoon classes ended, we had to return to the gym. However, this time it was for actual practice. During the hour of non-stop drills, I could hardly focus on anything except being tired. Our performance was a joke, and lifting afterward was an even bigger laugh. Guys were nearly crawling on the floor, and our bodies were too exhausted to lift the weights. We did our best to push through, though.

By 9 o'clock in the evening, when study hall was over, I couldn't keep my eyes open. I was tired from the overly strenuous day, and the saddest part of all was that I had to wake up at 5:30 a.m. the next morning to do it all over again.

Boot camp was turning out to be a vicious cycle, and for the most part, it drudged along slowly. The workouts were tough, but we got through them as a team. However, as we got into the second week, Coach Gillispie decided to treat us to a little extra conditioning in the afternoon. It was a nightmare…

He cut practice short one day to leave a little time for us to run sprints. He made us pair up in groups to run team line touches, also known as suicides. Even though our bodies were worn out, we offered no excuses. If Coach G had a time in mind, we had to make that time, no questions asked. Unfortunately, this particular time, the harder we ran, the further we fell behind the time and the longer we had to keep sprinting. None of us could make the time. The goal was for each pair to make two suicides in less than a minute.

I remember the sprints like they were yesterday; I matched up with the new freshman, Patrick Patterson. After all the continuous back and forth running, we all felt like we were about to keel over in exhaustion, but Patrick seemed to be in a little more pain than the rest of us. We were dealing with burning lungs and legs, while he was trying to fight through the newly formed blisters on his feet. They were so blistered that the skin on the bottom of his feet began peeling off in clumps. Disgustingly, his shoes were filled with blood. His white team socks had turned red.

He was hesitant to sit out, but the pain had to be excruciating. I had to run double but was happy to do so, considering the condition Patrick was in. Running double didn't let me escape an earful from Coach though, as he let me and the rest of the team know that I finished last. All I could do was laugh in between my gasps for air. It seemed helpful to maintain a sense of humor throughout the intense conditioning, especially heading into the final stretch of boot camp.

The last two days of boot camp were the worst. We had to run 22's, which consisted of running from baseline to baseline twice in 22 seconds, 22 times. For most basketball programs, that was the toughest thing you had to do, but under Coach G, we also had to run 35 suicides the following day. It was probably one of the most difficult experiences I'd ever been through. It blew the previous year's conditioning out of the water.

Of course, it was difficult to finish out the brutal demands of boot camp both mentally and physically, but after the final sprint, at that very moment, we had never felt closer as a team. We had survived together. Pushing through the pain and exhaustion was something for each of us to be proud of.

• • •

After two years of waiting, Big Blue Madness was finally in sight. All I had to do was get through another week of afternoon workouts, and I would be able to run out on the court and play in front of 23,000 screaming fans. The thought was almost too much for me to handle. It was so close I could taste it.

Thankfully, Coach Gillispie gave us the weekend after boot camp off. Monday brought the first of only three practices I had to make it through until I would be enjoying the festivities of Madness. All I had to do was practice hard and play injury free. A bit foreshadowing if you ask me.

Ten minutes into the practice that Monday, I felt a sharp pain in my foot. It was severe pain, but I fought through it. After what we had been through during boot camp, my foot was no problem at all. I just hoped the pain would pass with a good night's rest and plenty of treatment. So that evening I went back to the dorm and soaked my foot in a bucket of ice so it would be ready for the rest of the week's practices.

The following day I got my foot taped up tightly to help ease the pain. The trainer thought it was nothing more than a strained muscle, considering the fact that I had finished up practice the day before. The tape would help immobilize the foot when I ran, jumped, and cut to the basket during the course of practice.

As one could have easily guessed it, the tape didn't do anything to help my situation. To my horror, at the beginning of practice, I heard a loud pop in my foot while cutting back toward the basket. It was a sickening sound that turned my stomach inside out, and pain quickly followed. I knew immediately that my foot was in bad shape. I couldn't put any pressure on it no matter how much I gritted my teeth and tried to push through it. It angered me, but the hurting in my foot caused me to limp off the court and into the training room.

I sat in pain on a table in the training room until practice was over. From there, I was driven to the hospital for an x-ray. The results only confirmed what I had feared all along. It clearly showed that the 3rd metatarsal had completely snapped in half. Even though it didn't surprise me, disappointment and heartache suffocated me as doctors placed a boot on my foot and a nurse came in to fit me for crutches.

The doctor said that it had been a stress fracture until it finally gave out and snapped in two, but none of that really mattered to me. I didn't care if it was bad luck or fate. All that remained certain was that I had to sit out during a vital part of the season.

What value did I add to the team as an injured walk-on? Would Coach even want to keep me around? Sadly, I was overcome with doubt about my future with the team heading back to the practice facility. I was unsure of the fate that waited for me there.

• • •

Surprisingly, upon arriving back at the Joe Craft Center, I realized I had nothing to be worried about. Coach Gillispie was there to greet me with a pat on the shoulder.

He assured me with comforting words, "Don't worry about it, Krebs. You're going to be all right. Don't worry about anything except healing. You'll be back before you know it."

Even though I was upset about not participating in Big Blue Madness and was unable to compete for playing time early in the season, I was comforted by the assurance that my spot on the team was safe. I even remained optimistic when our team physician called to explain that I would need surgery on my foot. Although the idea of surgery frightened me, I trusted the doctor's opinion and diagnosis. All that was left for me to do was prepare for the operation and pray for a speedy recovery. Having my mom and dad in town certainly helped the process.

Interestingly enough, the surgery gave my body all sorts of new hardware. To foster healing and relieve pressure on the broken bone, doctors placed six screws and two plates in my foot. I was told post-surgery that it would take ten weeks to heal. That was too long.

A few days later during my check-up at the hospital, I asked the doctor, "Is it possible for me to be back before the ten weeks if I follow your orders and fight through the pain?"

The doctor responded, "It all depends on how fast your bones heal. I have no control over that aspect, but if you follow the advice of your trainer and me, there's a possibility that you could come back sooner. Of course, there are no guarantees of that."

I would miss a lot of the early games sitting out ten weeks, and that was unacceptable. I was determined to make it back for the North Carolina game. In my heart, something told me I would be back by then, but that only gave me seven weeks to recover from surgery. I had some serious work to do.

• • •

Unfortunately, my injury was only the beginning of many injuries for the team. Derrick Jasper, Ramon Harris, and Jodi Meeks were all injured at various times throughout the season. The injuries caused Coach to create different starting lineups for each game. This lack of flow caused our team to get off to a rocky start.

The loss to Gardner Webb in only the second game of the season was devastating to the players and UK fans everywhere. Not only did it get us started off on the wrong foot, but we also missed out on a chance to play at Madison Square Garden in New York. I hated sitting helpless on the sidelines just like always, dressed in a shirt, tie, and nice dress slacks. Although I had a big boot on my left foot this time, we were still losing games, and I still had not put on the Kentucky uniform. Frustration was beginning to mount.

That loss to Gardner Webb didn't accomplish too much, but it did motivate me to get better. It led me to believe that maybe I could help the team. But before I could do any of that, my foot needed to heal. In my situation, the only thing to do was continue to follow the doctor's orders and work hard during rehab so I could get back sooner rather than later.

Again, I looked to my mom's life for inspiration. Overcoming adversity was something I had learned from watching her daily battle against the malicious cancer in her body. Through her fight, she taught me to stay positive and remain focused on my goals. And my number-one goal was making the game against North Carolina my first game in a Kentucky uniform.

After pushing through intense pain and strenuous workouts to get my body back in basketball shape, I was able to accomplish that goal. I had worked my entire life for that moment and had been chasing the dream for over two years. Emotions started flooding my senses, and I almost didn't want to put the uniform on. Sitting in a chair in front of my locker, I remained fixated on the jersey that hung before me. And after taking a few moments to soak in the experience, I realized I had made it. Just like I'd imagined, dressing for the first time in my uniform was incredible. The opportunity to be playing against the University of North Carolina with my name on the back of my jersey was an indescribable joy.

It didn't take long for another unbelievable moment to come a few games later against Florida International on New Year's Eve. Since we were ahead 40 points, it seemed the lead was safe enough for me to check into the game.

Honestly, I didn't care if it was a tie game or a blowout, stepping on the court for the first time was an absolute thrill. All the hard work I had put in was finally paying off. It was amazing to think about all the things I had experienced as a Wildcat, and this marked the first time I had ever stepped foot on the court. Being on the court was enough for me, but magic was about to take place with under a minute to play in the game.

After making a few trips up and down the court, the ball ended up in my hands. Of all the places, it was right in front of our bench. Realizing I was open after coming off a screen, I jumped up and released the ball toward the basket. I watched intently as it traveled through the air. It looked good the entire way. My first shot as a Kentucky Wildcat was nothing but net! What was left of the crowd went crazy, and inside, I went crazy, too.

• • •

Although I was living out my dream in every sense of the word, the season itself began as a huge disappointment. After the Gardner Webb defeat, we also lost to UAB, Houston, and San Diego. In addition, we were beaten in every rival game. North Carolina, Indiana, and Louisville all gave us more than we could handle. Our record near the end of non-conference play was a dismal six wins and seven losses.

The mood around Lexington was not a positive one, and there was no excitement around campus. Sadly, it became difficult to find the motivation to win. The team was frustrated and injured heading into SEC play. It was going to take some serious soul-searching to get everything back on track, but nothing was impossible.

Amazingly, even in the face of so many obstacles and distractions, we found the courage to turn the season around. We started out on fire during SEC play. We knocked off ranked opponents like Vanderbilt and Tennessee to jump-start our winning streak. Even though each game was a dogfight, we found it inside of us to pull out a victory.

On a personal level, I saw action in three conference games against Georgia, Mississippi State, and Florida at key moments in each of those games.

We would be down by three points at the end of the game when Coach G would call out, "Krebs, go in!"

It was an incredible rush being thrust into the game at those moments. It was even more incredible that with only three games left before the SEC tournament, we stood at nine wins and four losses.

As we finished out the season, the team's energy was high, Coach G was pleased, and fans were happy. Everything seemed to be going our way, but just like most things that season, the good times wouldn't last long. Every season has its ups and downs, but this season definitely saw more trials than tribulations.

With only three games left in the season, we got news that Patrick Patterson would have to miss the rest of the season due to a foot injury. He was our inside force, and we needed him to win. This news was a blow to the gut of our team.

Luckily, Ramel Bradley and Joe Crawford carried the extra weight on their shoulders, along with critical contributions from Perry Stevenson, to finish out the season on an upswing. We won the last three games without Patrick and finished with twelve wins and four losses in the SEC. Considering we started the season out with six wins and seven losses, the turn around we made was spectacular, and each member of the team was excited for tournament time.

• • •

The 2008 Southeastern Conference Tournament took place in Atlanta, Georgia. Since the season had ended so well, excitement filled the air. As a team, we were very positive even though Patrick wasn't going to be on the court with us.

Because of our stellar run in SEC play, we had a bye the first round. When Georgia won their first-round game, we realized they were going to be our first opponent. The city became electrified with excitement about the upcoming game.

As we stood in the locker room preparing for our battle against the Georgia Bulldogs, the unthinkable happened. The second-round game had to be postponed.

During our pregame talk from Coach Gillispie with only 40 minutes left before tipoff, a thunderous roar from the crowd overcame the Georgia Dome. It wasn't because of an amazing play or a poor call from the officials. No, it was because a tornado had struck the dome and ripped a hole in the roof. The fans in attendance were scared for their lives.

Not knowing what was happening, each member of the team feared for family that was out in the crowd. We had no idea the extent of the damage because we were stuck in our locker room.

After hours of deliberation and sitting on a bus in the back of the Georgia Dome, the game was postponed until the following day at noon. And because of the hole in the roof, the game had to be played at Georgia Tech.

With all the commotion, we didn't get back to our hotel and in bed until 2 a.m. To follow our usual pregame routine, we had to wake up at 7 a.m. the next morning for our team shoot around. It was tough to stay focused with all that had happened, but it remained vital to keep our minds on the game.

We didn't realize the biggest disappointment of the whole situation until we actually got to the game. The 20,000 Kentucky fans who had come to Atlanta to watch us play weren't going to be able to attend the game. Only school officials and guests of the players were allowed inside the facility. The circumstances seemed to get worse and worse.

To top it all off, after a hard-fought game down to the wire, we lost on a last-second 3-pointer to the Georgia Bulldogs. After the game, the only thing we could do was gather our composure and cross our fingers for a berth into the NCAA Tournament. We refused to believe our season would come to an end like that. It was important to stay positive until we learned our fate during the selection show on Sunday after the conclusion of the conference tournaments. For my mind's sake, that show couldn't come fast enough.

When Sunday finally rolled around, we were all invited over to Coach Gillispie's house to watch the NCAA Tournament Selection Show. Everyone in the house made small talk awaiting the verdict of getting into the tournament. After eating dinner together as a team, we piled around the television to find out our future. Uneasiness filled the house until they announced that Kentucky had received an 11-seed. We were off to Anaheim, California, to play Marquette in the first round.

With this announcement came excitement and the relief of a fresh start. None of the other games made a difference anymore. For the time being, we were in the big dance and could still win the National Championship. Odds were mounted against us, but crazy things always happen in the tournament.

● ● ●

We landed in California with hopes of overcoming all our personal obstacles and surpassing people's expectations. I, for one, was excited about experiencing my first NCAA tournament. It was a childhood dream in and of itself.

However, right before the game, as I finished my pre-game meal with sights set on a first-round win, I was informed that I wasn't going to be able to sit on the bench. There were too many assistant coaches, managers, and players to all fit on the bench so I had to be one of the players to step away.

I was crushed.

Apparently, my broken foot and missing part of the season was the rationale, but it still didn't make sense. What about the work I had put in to return earlier than expected? I felt embarrassed, depressed, and insane to have put in as much work as I had only to be told I couldn't play with my team when it really mattered. It hurt to know I wasn't needed, and it hurt even more to watch us lose in the first round of the 2008 NCAA Tournament.

• • •

After losing against Marquette, Coach G called the players, managers, and staff together for a meeting back at the hotel. The gathering was to let the seniors know how everyone felt about them. It was a way to tell them good-bye on a positive note. Every one of us had an opportunity to say something about each senior and about the fond memories of the past season.

This meeting also brought a light of understanding to Coach Gillispie. He undeniably had a different style of coaching, and his methods for preparing us for the high level of play was unusual, but it was evident that he truly cared about each and every one of us.

Is it true that he didn't let us warm up before one game because he believed we had already disgraced the uniform enough? Yes. He was so upset at the game before that refused to let us on the court until twenty minutes before tip-off.

Did he say no one was going to make the trip to Florida except the five starters? Yes. I remember we all went to his office and sat there before our bus left from the Joe Craft Center to the airport. We gathered in his office like a surprise birthday party to beg him to take us on the trip. He eventually ended up letting us go.

Did he have tough practices on game days? Sometimes. There were days when he would make us run the stairs at Rupp Arena, and there were days we wouldn't even break a sweat.

I always liked to believe there were reasons for the things he did, and the meeting after the tournament loss hinted that I was right. It gave me and the rest of the team a chance to see another side of Coach

## I was still determined to improve the state of the team

Gillispie. He let his guard down a little. He told each of us what we meant to him.

Even though I was angry about not being on the bench for the biggest game of my life, I was still determined to improve the state of the team in the future. Ever since I was young, I had an image of what Kentucky Basketball was all about. An 11-seed wasn't it, and I wanted to be part of the team that brought Kentucky Basketball back to greatness.

After our meeting at the hotel came to an end, I boarded the plane filled with determination as we headed back east to Lexington.

# 9

# CHARACTER
## Another Coach Here and Gone

The Marquette game was still fresh in our minds as we did our best to transition from one season to another. Unfortunately, though, before we could begin worrying about the season ahead, heartbreak struck the university and Kentucky fans everywhere. The NCAA Tournament defeat wasn't the biggest loss we would experience during that time of year.

It was only a few weeks after my sophomore season came to an end in Anaheim that tragedy hit the program hard. The news got to me when I received a call late one night from a friend in the media department at UK.

After a few minutes of small talk, he continued on in an unusually somber tone, "Have you heard about Mr. Keightley?"

I honestly had no idea what he was talking about. It sounded as if something awful had happened to our long-time equipment manager and heart of Kentucky Basketball for nearly 50 years, Bill Keightley.

My friend went on to say, "He isn't doing well. He went up to see a Cincinnati Reds baseball game and fell sick during the trip. They immediately took him to the hospital. I don't have many details right now, but I'm overhearing a lot of people talking about it. I'll call you back if I hear anything else."

After the conversation concluded, I hung up the phone in shock.

Ten minutes later, I received the call back with news that Mr. Keightley had passed away. We lost him in April of 2008.

I didn't know all the details about how he had passed or why such an amazing man would be taken from this earth so unexpectedly, but I was incredibly upset at the idea of his being gone. I knew it was an enormous loss to the team, the university, and the community as a whole, but most of all, I felt for his family, for his wife.

He was a great man and a joy to be around. He was a close friend and confidant to everyone who had ever met him. Mr. Keightley was our "go to" man, especially for Coach Gillispie. He and Coach were particularly close, and the loss hit him extremely hard. There was no doubt in my mind: It was going to take a long time for the program to cope with this tragic loss.

Needless to say, Mr. Keightley's funeral was very emotional. He had touched an incredible number of people in his life. John Pelphrey, a former UK player and head coach of Arkansas; Rick Pitino, now head coach at Louisville; and Coach Tubby Smith, head coach at Minnesota, were all present at his funeral. And thousands of others made the trip back to Lexington to say good-bye to a truly remarkable man.

Sadly, losing Mr. Keightley wasn't the only change in the spring. The end of the school year also brought a lot of different modifications to the roster. Derrick Jasper transferred to UNLV, Mark Coury left for Cornell, and Morakinyo Williams went home to England until he found another school. Seniors Joe Crawford and Ramel Bradley graduated and would be greatly missed. Every change brought more uncertainty about my upcoming junior season at Kentucky.

• • •

Throughout the month of May, so many different names flooded the roster until there were about 20 players on the team. I was thankful for each and every one of the new additions, but I couldn't help but wonder, how many players is too many? How can a team of 20 players function as one unit?

As I thought about each of the new recruits, I noticed a random coincidence about the past couple of seasons, and although it isn't crucial to my story, I share it here because if nothing else, it's quite interesting. In 2005, Coach Smith signed a scholarship player named Adam Williams who chose the number 25, stayed only one year, and then transferred. In 2007, Morakinyo Williams joined the team under Coach Gillispie. He was another scholarship player who wore the number 25 and then transferred after one year. At this point, Donald Williams was going to be a new scholarship player on the 2008-2009 team, and, you guessed it, he also picked the number 25. I couldn't help thinking it would be awfully strange if, in the period of four years, UK signed three scholarship players, each with the last name Williams, each wearing the number 25, and each playing for one year and then transferring. (HINT: It actually happens).

Now back to the end of my sophomore year at UK. Heading into summer workouts, I was apprehensive at best. But despite all the changes that had occurred, I did my best to remain upbeat. It seemed more useful to worry about things I could control. So my conditioning and strength training moved to the top of my priority list.

Typically, running began at 6 o'clock each morning. It seemed impossible, but the workouts were much more difficult than the previous year. The conditioning was strenuous, and many times after practice, I found myself unable to function throughout the rest of the day.

We would head to the indoor football stadium and do about 40 timed 100-yard sprints. Coach Forcier, the Strength and Conditioning Coach, would have us run up and down the concrete steps of the football stadium. If, by chance, we happened to stay in the practice facility, we would do various agility exercises that were tiring in a totally different way. In addition, weightlifting was a daily complement to the overwhelming conditioning regimen.

Deep down, I knew the key to my development as an athlete was my drive to excel through any workout, regardless of how demanding it happened to be. The faster I embraced this, the better.

Finally, after what seemed like never-ending mornings of incredibly challenging workouts, tough conditioning didn't bother me anymore. It became my mission to be in better shape than I was the year before. Getting in top shape during the preseason meant I could focus more on improving my basketball skills than on being tired when boot camp rolled around in October.

To be honest, I was thrilled with the progression I had made in one year. My bench press went from 185 pounds for 3 reps to between 14 and 16 reps in only a few months. Understandably, I was excited for the start of the school year because I was stronger, faster, and better conditioned than ever before.

• • •

Working hard throughout the summer made the months fly by. Before I knew it, my family was moving me back into the Wildcat Lodge for the start of classes in August. And I was ready for it this time. I knew what to expect and what was expected of me.

I had built this confidence through intense hours in the gym preparing for anything Coach G could happen to throw my way. In fact, boot camp no longer intimidated me. Instead, my focus changed to helping the new players excel through the three-a-day workouts. It dawned on me that I was a veteran now and could help the young guys by giving them key tips on how to approach the horrors of boot camp.

To my benefit, I maintained a positive attitude during the two weeks of boot camp, and it allowed me to do extremely well throughout the long days of intense workouts. Thinking about my teammates and using the knowledge I had gained over the course of the year under Coach G helped me see – and feel – the preseason as much less extreme than I had the previous year. As a result, after months of dedication and hard work, I was prepared to contribute to the team all throughout the 2008-2009 season.

• • •

Before I knew it, Big Blue Madness was right around the corner, and this year it happened to fall right on my 22nd birthday, October 10, 2008. I was finally in position to experience the festivities of Madness firsthand (since, thanks to my broken foot, I'd been sidelined the entire first part of last season).

So much had happened in my time at Kentucky, but I still had yet to participate in Big Blue Madness.

It was hard to believe how far I had come since my move from Thomas More to UK, but the roar of 23,000 fans that erupted when the announcer introduced me, "6'5" Junior, from Newport, Kentucky, Mark Krebs," was a reminder that I had made it.

**it felt good to give them something to cheer about**

As I stood waving to the crowd, realizing my mom, dad, and entire family were there watching, I knew in my heart that they were as excited as I was. My family's never-ending support was what got me to this point in my life, and after all we had been through together, it felt good to give them something to cheer about.

Unfortunately, the excitement and support wasn't quite enough to start the season out with a win. Just like the previous season, we slipped up coming out of the gate and lost our first game to VMI. We scored more than 100 points at home and still managed to lose. And the worst part was that we had to start a whole new season with the same crushing feeling of defeat we'd suffered through last season.

With that blow to the gut, the team's morale was drained. The season's beginning dragged on as we struggled to make up ground. Even though we ended up winning the tournament in Las Vegas, defeating both Kansas State and West Virginia, there was still no energy, no desire to win. Instead of hitting mid-season with a bang, we looked like we were running out of gas, and it was only the beginning of non-conference play. Something definitely needed to change if we wanted to become a competitive team in the SEC.

• • •

The one high point (if you can call it a high point) of this sluggish beginning was that we actually got off to a better start than we had the previous year. It took a few wins after the tournament in Las Vegas to get the wheels rolling. We had an impressive winning streak going until losses began finding us in the most devastating ways.

The 2008-2009 season truly was a year full of heartbreak. We lost numerous games on last-second shots. The moment we thought we had a game in our grasp, the other team ripped it from our hands. Even the game at Louisville ended with a near-half-court shot to put the Cardinals ahead as the final buzzer sounded.

It was a bitter truth, but over the years, I'd been forced to learn how to keep things in perspective. So although the Louisville game made me miserable, I had other things playing in my mind.

Case and point, I recall the bus ride home after the Louisville game. I remained composed and fought back the negative emotions of losing a huge rivalry game the way we did. I wanted so badly to just get mad and give into my urges of focusing on how awful I felt inside. However, my mind was once again on my mom. I had no time for even the slightest bit of selfishness because she had another big surgery to overcome, and it was scheduled for the morning after our return from Louisville.

It started a few weeks earlier when she was scheduled for a routine MRI to check up on the status of her cancer. Sadly, the doctors found a rather large tumor on her spine, and it was pressing on her spinal cord. Not only was it causing excruciating pain, but if surgery wasn't performed, there was a great chance she could become paralyzed. If the tumor continued to grow and broke through the cord, death would be eminent. After years of having cancer eat away at her body and withstanding nearly 300 intravenous chemotherapy treatments, my mom was broken down and weak. The risks involved with a person in her condition going through major surgery made the operation even more challenging.

Luckily, Coach Gillispie understood the severity of the situation. He was very sympathetic and encouraged me to go right home after we arrived back in Lexington. He told me not to worry about practices until my mom recovered and assured me that he would be praying for her through this difficult time.

I followed Coach Gillispie's orders and made the drive home so that I could spend a few hours with my mom before she went to bed. Knowing the gravity of her situation, I cherished every second we spent together that night. After all, it could have been the last moments my mom and I shared. The operation was going to be another intense battle for her to fight.

• • •

When it came time for surgery, I remember sitting anxiously in the waiting room for several long and grueling hours. I kept thinking to myself that my mom had a bunch more living to do. By no means was she ready to leave this earth. Positive thoughts about her laughter and smile comforted me as I waited for the surgery to be over. The clock moved slowly all day. The lack of updates from the nurses in the operating room made minutes feel like hours.

Finally, after what seemed like an eternity, the surgeon came out and spoke with us. He discussed what went on during the delicate procedure. My family crammed into his office to hear the news.

He explained, "The tumor was removed and a reinforcing rod was put into her spine. The big concern now will be seeing if she can use her legs. Sometimes when the patient awakes from surgery, the nerves and spinal cord don't work properly and paralysis can set in. However, I am confident she will walk again post-surgery. The biggest concern for us was that her heart wasn't strong enough for surgery, but she proved us wrong on that end. You can all rest easy now, she is stable in recovery."

Another hour ticked slowly by on the clock before we could actually see her. They wanted the anesthetic to wear off before visitors were allowed at her bedside. When we finally approached my mom's bed, her eyes opened wide, and a smile formed across her face as she laid eyes on my dad and her children. We all gave her a hug and told her how happy we were that she was safely out of the operating room.

Luckily, my mom had survived the surgery and was, above all else, alive with more time to experience life. As time passed, my mom regained her ability to walk. She had some difficulty and had to use a cane, but with time and patience, she was able to get around on her own once again.

The only bit of independence she actually lost was the ability to drive a car. My mom was never one to depend on others, but she learned to accept her fate over time. As a family, we were glad to take on any of the burden, and she knew she could rely on us. It was amazing to see the will, determination, and drive she had to get her life back as close to normal as possible.

The rapid nature of my mom's recovery was impressive to witness. The doctors were perplexed. With as much cancer that remained throughout her body and the vast amounts of chemotherapy, the healing process should be slow and gradual at best. However, my mom was up and walking within a week of having her spine cut open and worked on.

Not only was her quick recovery a huge blessing that my family got to experience firsthand, but it also allowed me to rejoin my team at UK in time for the start of our SEC schedule.

Despite our mediocre non-conference play, we started off on fire and won the first five SEC games we played. During one of those early wins, Jodie Meeks, a fellow junior guard, broke Dan Issle's UK record for most points in a game. He scored 54 points with 10 three-pointers in a road win against Tennessee. On national television, he gave the performance of a lifetime, and it was by far the best performance I had ever seen from a single player in all my life.

Unfortunately, after such a fantastic start, a string of tough losses began. After the first loss to Ole Miss, it was like someone pulled the plug from the drain, and the season went spiraling downward. I can't pinpoint the exact moment, but somewhere during the middle of SEC play, things fell apart. Team morale sunk and our positive attitude went south. We got complacent as a team, and frustration began eating away at our cohesiveness. The South Carolina and LSU games were both lost on last-second shots.

After starting 5-0, we went 3-11 to close out the season, and we ended up with 8 wins and 8 losses in conference play. There was no way we could make the NCAA Tournament unless we won the SEC Tournament. Our performance in Tampa, FL. was going to determine the fate of our season.

• • •

Like everyone else involved with the program, I wasn't immune to the frustration of such a horrible losing streak.

The incessant reminders of, "Krebs, be ready to play. We're going to need you today," from Coach Gillispie began eating away at my composure.

I grew uncharacteristically angry because it was clear he never actually planned on putting me in the game. It all toyed with my emotions, and it was a terrible letdown every single time I believed him. Needless to say, I was tired of the disappointment.

But despite the frustration, I still found myself going to the gym late at night and putting in extra work. It was like a bad habit, but I never knew when my name might really be called, so I wanted to stay prepared.

During one particularly late-night shooting session, I decided to try and dunk the ball. I never knew I could even come close to throwing one down, but surprisingly, that night I discovered that dunking the ball was something I could do. I started out with one-handed dunks off one foot, then two hands off two feet, and quickly escalated into reverse dunks and 360s. The next day after practice, my teammates cheered me on as I proved to all of them that I could indeed dunk. It was a shocking transformation overnight and unbelievable to people who weren't there to witness it.

I relied on my new athletic abilities to provide me with a little motivation to close out the season because our game performances certainly weren't cutting it. The 2009 SEC Tournament in Tampa didn't go much better for us than the close of the regular season. We lost in the second round to LSU.

After the game, we waved good-bye to any chance of making the NCAA Tournament. I just couldn't wrap my mind around the idea that we were NIT bound after we'd had such a promising start.

Back in Lexington, Coach Gillispie made us watch the NCAA Tournament Selection Show as a team anyway. It was brutal. We knew, as well as Coach, that our only hope after such a disastrous season was to win the SEC Tournament, and we failed horribly at accomplishing that goal. So each of us sat dejectedly around Wildcat Lodge watching other schools make the NCAA Tournament.

After all the hard work we'd put in during the previous year, it seemed like a nightmare that the season would end up like it did. I couldn't bear to watch the television as team after team was called to fill out the bracket for the 2009 NCAA Tournament. Kentucky was nowhere on the list.

• • •

The only bright spot throughout the NIT was that once again we had terrific fan support. We didn't really want to be there because we had lost control of a season that had so much potential, but the fans made the journey worthwhile. Playing in a jam-packed Memorial Coliseum against UNLV was enough for me.

However, after beating UNLV and Creighton, the season came to a crashing halt against Notre Dame in the third round.

Not long after the loss, all the speculation and hearsay became reality as Coach Gillispie was fired. Unlike the private nature of Coach Smith's departure, Coach Gillispie's firing seemed to happen almost publicly. As a result, we weren't totally surprised by the decision. Throughout the latter part of the season, whispers of his impending firing followed us wherever we went. It was difficult to fathom another new coach taking over at Kentucky.

The media frenzy, the legal battle, and the string of never-ending changes were awful. It was such a nasty situation. Even though the prospect of having a new coach intrigued Kentucky fans everywhere, I was left with scary thoughts about not being able to finish out my college basketball career. Moreover, I was afraid my career would end with no significance at all. As an 8-seed in 2007, an 11-seed in 2008, and an NIT bid in 2009, our team was barely surviving through the dark ages of Kentucky Basketball. Even though I had fulfilled my dream of playing at UK, the team had hit one of its lowest points in history. Everything I'd accomplished personally seemed tainted.

Were my three years in a Kentucky uniform a huge waste of my time?

I knew the answer to that question in my heart. No matter how my career played out, I could never see it as a waste. The friendships and experiences I'd had throughout my time at Kentucky were priceless. So instead of wallowing in self-pity, I stayed optimistic that someone would resurrect the program. I just hoped the new coach would let me be around to help make it happen.

• • •

Luckily, around the time of all the chaos, I was presented with the perfect distraction from all the worrying about my future at UK.

On March 30, 2009, my niece, Peyton Marie Hester, was born. Mandy and Neal had a beautiful daughter, and my mom now had a precious granddaughter. She was there during the delivery, actually holding Mandy's hand through it all. I can't imagine the joy my mom

> **...the tough times helped me learn a little something about my character**

felt in knowing that she was accomplishing more and more of the goals she set for herself. They were goals that had kept her alive for so long. All the pain she endured for nearly eight years was paying off. Step by step, my mom was walking with us through the journey of life: birthdays, anniversaries, graduations, and now, the birth of a grandchild.

After reflecting on my mother's situation and what she had gone through to experience important milestones in life, I thought about the strength of my family. Thinking back at how we came together during the tough times helped me learn a little something about my own personal character.

I had become a stronger person mentally and emotionally because of my mother's ongoing fight with cancer and the turmoil I experienced with Kentucky Basketball.

Even so, a third coach in four years was coming into the program, and I would once again have to prove myself to someone new. Beyond all else, my work ethic and drive to succeed would be tested yet again.

I realized then that character isn't built from the smooth times in life. On the contrary, it's built from the adversity and challenges

> **How we overcome obstacles defines our character**

we face when things aren't going the way we want them to. How we overcome obstacles defines our character, and my character, along with my unyielding determination, had prepared me to leap over any barriers in the way of achieving the rest of my dream.

# MY JOURNEY
## Mark Krebs

My first portrait

Me as a newborn dealing with kidney problems.

My big sister welcoming me as her little brother

Our new addition to the family, Andrew

The Family

8th grade basketball

High school basketball

Mom sporting her new wig

Senior Night

Christmas time with
our golden retriever, Nala

I'll never forget what this night meant

25th wedding anniversary and renewal of their vows

My sister's wedding - October 28th, 2006

Getting ready to check into my first game as a Kentucky Wildcat

Weeks before her first spine surgery

Peyton's Baptism

Mom reached yet another milestone, enjoying precious moments with her granddaughter, Peyton Marie

At the Kentucky Derby
with 4-year manager, Chad
Sanders, and teammate,
Patrick Patterson

Brothers
together
at UK

The locker room at Rupp Arena

John Wall celebrating my throw down at Big Blue Madness

My final game at Rupp Arena - Senior Day

Me and Patrick going crazy after my three-pointer against Wake Forest in the second round of the NCAA Tournament

The team going crazy after my three-pointer against Wake Forest
in the second round of the NCAA Tournament

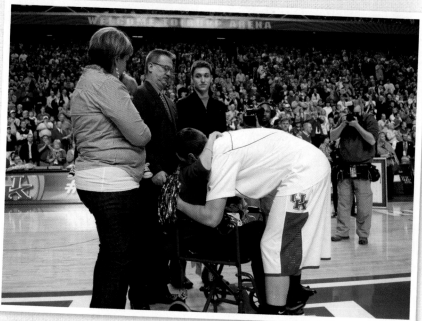

Embracing my mom at midcourt on Senior Day

Holding back tears during the playing of My Old Kentucky Home

# 10

# FAITH
## Coach Cal Arrives

The same lost and lonely feeling I felt two years earlier was back. I spent most of my days contemplating whether or not I would be invited to return for my senior season. I hated the uncertainty. What new coach coming into an elite program, needing to make an immediate impact, would want a walk-on who had barely stepped foot on the court?

I personally knew I had a lot to offer. I was dedicated, hard working, and a valuable teammate, but I couldn't offer anything that would jump off the page to an incoming coach who didn't know where I'd come from or what I'd already brought to the team. I knew that whoever took charge would probably flip directly to the statistics to see the playing time of each player. Where would that leave me?

I hated the in-between periods of trying to figure out who our next leader was going to be. Each day someone new seemed to be considered for the job. The news was littered with information about who would be the best candidate. Donovan, Pelphrey, Ford, and Calipari were among the leading contenders.

All I wanted to do was finish out my career, but I also understood the magnitude of the situation the university faced. They needed someone exceptional to fill the shoes of an ambassador, role model, and national icon for the university and the state of Kentucky as a whole. With all the worrying came a flood of different emotions. I was scared that I wouldn't get to play my senior season, but I was also eager to prove myself to whoever became my third coach in just four years.

It was vital for me to stay positive through the selection process, so I made the decision to accept whatever situation I was given. And, lucky for me, it seemed like the less fretting I did about the current state of affairs, the clearer everything became. It didn't matter who came our way; I would be ready.

It wasn't long before all the signs pointed to one man to be our next coach. He was an extremely successful man, and from the looks of it on television, his teams had a blast playing for him. They were always the fastest, strongest, and most athletic in the country. They sprinted on fast breaks every trip down the court. Alley-oops and rim-rattling dunks were commonplace on his teams.

Eventually, it seemed as if every news station, newspaper, and sports show knew the name of the new coach, but still nothing was official.

• • •

As I awoke on one bright and beautiful spring morning, I rolled over to quiet the incessant beeping of my cell phone. It was alerting me of an incoming text message.

I flipped the phone open to read the following words, "Meeting at 9 a.m. in the lodge with your new coach, John Calipari."

It was just as everyone had suspected, but, as a player, I was happy to finally know for sure. I knew from day one that he would be the best for the job. He was exceptional with the media, a true people person, and the epitome of a player's coach. With all of these amazing qualities, he was going to be an incredibly difficult person to prove myself to. John Calipari had been in the business a long time, and there was probably nothing he hadn't seen already.

Once again, I convinced myself that none of that mattered; I had to stay confident and focused.

As each of the returning players sat in the kitchen of Wildcat Lodge, whispers of excitement filled the air about what to expect when Coach Calipari walked through the door.

Flashbacks of Coach Gillispie walking through the Lodge doors for the first time two years ago ran through my mind. I remembered the overwhelming sensation I'd felt, and I recalled each and every word he'd spoken. It was such an eerie feeling to know we'd all been here before.

Thankfully, it wasn't long before Coach Cal entered the room and the whispers promptly turned to silence. Grins covered each face as everyone in the room sat fixated on the man who'd been sent to resurrect our team from the doldrums. One by one, we stood up to shake the hand of our new leader.

As a player, I appreciated the fact that Coach Calipari appeared to be the most excited person in the room. He explained to each of us that coaching at Kentucky was his dream job. He made it clear that we were going to have a blast playing the game of basketball for him.

Coach went on to discuss what the season was typically like for his teams, touching on the topics that were of particular interest to the returning players, such as practices, coaching style, and rules. It was all music to my ears. He was emotional but also encouraging, and he said all the right things. There wouldn't be any intense practices before games, and the only thing he asked is that we behaved as men.

By the time he left our meeting, I knew I'd never wanted to play basketball as badly as I did at that moment.

• • •

Shortly after our initial team meeting came to a close, Coach was ready for his press conference. It should come as no surprise that the fans absolutely adored him. His charismatic and smooth way of speaking mesmerized the onlookers. The hiring of Coach Calipari revived the city of Lexington. Within a few hours, the entire atmosphere on campus changed, and by the end of the press conference, ripples of excitement spread throughout the state and across the country. Kentucky Basketball needed a change, and this was exactly the transformation everyone had hoped for.

I wanted so badly to be unselfish and happy about all that was happening, but I was undeniably nervous about my personal status on the team. I'd heard that Coach Calipari didn't traditionally have walk-ons, and, as I looked at our current roster, I noticed that we had five. Would we all have to fight for one spot? Would we all be asked to move on and leave the team? Would he keep only the seniors? There were so many questions racing through my mind, but I once again reminded myself that some things just aren't meant to be controlled. So instead of worrying, I remained faithful that all my hard work would not go unnoticed.

• • •

It wasn't long before I'd have a chance to prove my worthiness to Coach Calipari. Because he was so excited about the journey ahead, he didn't waste any time jumping into spring practices. He couldn't wait to see what kind of team he'd been given. I felt the same excitement and was eager to start with a clean slate. Even though proving myself to another coach would be a grueling process, I was happy to have the opportunity for a fresh start.

The first workout under new management was a very unique one, to say the least. There were no assistant coaches to help with drills. Coach Cal was left alone to instruct and get acquainted with the 18 players remaining on our team, which was probably more than any other team in the country. In fact, it seemed more like a football team than a basketball team.

Nonetheless, the workout went smoothly from start to finish. Every drill of the workout was fun and competitive. Coach Cal was positive, energetic, and patient. At least for the first workout, he brought enjoyment back to the game. In essence, he was everything the returning players needed.

However, when the hour-long practice came to an end, I could sense that coach was a bit overwhelmed with trying to assess the talent of a team with so many players. (Who wouldn't be?) But despite being slightly overwhelmed, he never once lost his composure. The way he remained upbeat and optimistic amidst the trying circumstances was truly impressive.

It didn't take Coach long before he quickly realized it was impossible improve the team with so many players running around. When we met as a team before the next practice, he warned that all the walk-ons would have to stay off the court so he could more easily evaluate the scholarship players.

I felt sick to my stomach and feared I would never be able to step foot on the court again. I couldn't prove myself as a player without having the chance to play. I appreciated Coach's honesty, but it didn't ease the sense of despair that threatened to overwhelm me.

Luckily, my worrying came to an end when I found out that Michael Porter, another soon-to-be senior on the team, wasn't going to participate that day. Apparently, he'd met with Coach and decided to step away from basketball to focus on family life with his wife and newborn daughter. I was saddened by the fact that he would no longer be my teammate, but I also recognized his absence as an opportunity knocking at my door. After all, without Mike, there was an uneven number of scholarship players.

As practice began, I made the split-second decision to muster up enough courage to jump into practice with the scholarship guys. I figured the worst that could happen was Coach Cal telling me to stand on the sidelines. And I knew that if I played well enough, Coach wouldn't care if I were on scholarship or not.

The only thing I needed to do was back up my rash actions with a solid performance. As the saying goes, it was time to put my money where my mouth was.

Needless to say, I made an impression on him. My performance was strong, and from that point forward, I decided to quit panicking about my status on the team. Instead, I made a commitment to put all my cards on the table. I wanted to give everything I had so I wouldn't have any regrets – no matter what happened. Even if I didn't have a place in this new system, at least I gave it my all and didn't back down. I would be able to walk with my head held high and would accept the harsh truth that it just wasn't meant to be.

• • •

After trying my best to make an impact during the month of April, I got to spend the month of May at home with my family, just as the team had always done in the past. As players, we saw this little break as a chance for us to regroup and get ready for summer workouts. For me personally, it was an opportunity to spend an extended period of time at home, sharing invaluable moments with my mom.

This particular May marked the year of Andrew's graduation from Newport Central Catholic. Amazingly, my mom was able to reach yet another milestone: seeing her youngest son receive his high school diploma.

*This accomplishment signified that mom had fought the disease long enough to successfully raise all of her children past high school and into their years of independence. Had she let the disease consume her after the initial year, Andrew would have only been in 6th grade, I would have been merely a sophomore in high school, and Mandy would have just been beginning college. Now, seven years later, as Andrew walked across the stage in his blue cap and gown, each of us children knew how important it was for her to survive this long. We were able to have our mom through the most crucial stages of our development. This was truly remarkable to me.*

• • •

The month of May was also an important time for Kentucky Basketball. Throughout the spring, Coach Calipari signed on six new recruits for the following year. Kentucky's #1-ranked recruiting class in college basketball included top talent in the country like Eric Bledsoe, DeMarcus Cousins, Daniel Orton, and, at the very top of the list, John Wall.

The potential talent on the team was incredible, and there was no doubt I wanted to be part of it. However, I found myself at a crossroads and couldn't decide what to do. My brain was telling me to go ahead and finish up classes in the summer, save some money while getting my degree, and say farewell to basketball forever. But my heart was telling me to take the chance and finish out my senior year. I knew with every ounce of my soul that it was going to be a special season. But at the same time, I also knew it would cost me a fortune to finish up my degree requirements the next year while playing basketball – even though I needed only one more class to do so.

What if Coach told me to go home at the end of summer workouts anyway? Would it all be worth the risk?

All in all, these questions didn't take that much deliberation on my part. I remembered the words of my mom that had gotten me to Kentucky in the first place. Everything I would regret if I walked away from my dream entered my mind. Suddenly, I knew that compared to the experience I would cherish for a lifetime, money didn't matter at all. I was committed to remaining a Kentucky Wildcat and had faith that it would all work out in the end.

> **I was committed... and had faith that it would all work out in the end**

For the moment at least, it was encouraging to know I'd be back in Lexington come June with yet another opportunity to solidify a spot on the team. And looking at the roster, I would have a lot of work to do to accomplish that feat. Even so, I couldn't wait to see how the new incoming freshman meshed with all the returning players.

Taking everything into consideration, summer was shaping up to be something special.

• • •

Eager to meet all the newcomers, I almost couldn't wait to step foot on campus at the start of June. Even though the team was vastly different, I was pleased to see most of the walk-ons had made it back for summer workouts. Amazingly, out of the thirteen scholarship players we had the previous season, only six remained: Patrick Patterson, Ramon Harris, Perry Stevenson, Josh Harrellson, Darius Miller, and DeAndre Liggins. In addition, four of the five walk-ons also remained, myself included.

I quickly realized that Coach Calipari wasn't going to allow a roster of sixteen on his team, so my mission became to give everything I had, every single day of summer. Each time I saw an opening to improve, I went for it. For instance, even though walk-ons weren't required to wake up early and lift as a team under Coach Cal, I still joined in the lifts at 7 a.m. Our Strength and Conditioning Coach, Todd Forcier, actually encouraged me to do so because he believed I could help out the freshmen in the weight room. It was a role I gladly accepted.

I hungered to be a part of Kentucky's rise back to prominence in college basketball, and I wasn't going to do one thing to jeopardize my chances of returning to the team. My job was to work harder than everyone else, be a better teammate than I had ever been before, and offer the team an irreplaceable quality. I searched all summer to find my niche on the team.

• • •

One day, in the midst of my everyday battle to improve throughout the summer, the team was treated to a surprise. In the middle of one of our pickup games, Lebron James strolled into the gym to watch us play. Not only was I pleasantly surprised, but I was also excited about the relationship that soon developed between the University of Kentucky and "King" James. That day gave testament to the influence that Coach Calipari had in the realm of sports, and it strengthened my determination to succeed. I began thinking about all the other perks and surprises that might come next.

With excitement in the air, the hot summer months flew by. At the end of workouts in late July, I reached my moment of truth. I overheard the other walk-ons discussing how they each had an individual meeting with some of the assistant coaches later in the day. I personally had no idea what they were talking about because I hadn't received that message. I scoured through my text messages and missed calls, but there was nothing.

Should I take no news as good news? Was this simply a technology glitch? What could the meeting be about? I decided it was important to go to the meeting anyway, just in case.

On my way over to the basketball offices, I received a call that stopped me in my tracks. As I parked the car in front of the practice facility, I was informed that the walk-ons were let go. My heart nearly dropped out of my chest. I felt awful for my friends but also wondered if I was about to face that same fate.

Rushing into the offices, I entered the conference room where some of the staff still sat in discussion. Martin Newton, Director of Basketball Operations, welcomed me with a warm greeting and led me over to his office. As soon as we were seated comfortably at his desk, he began to explain everything to me.

Martin expressed his sorrow for the unfortunate situation the other walk-ons faced. However, in regards to me, he continued on in an enthusiastic tone.

He said, "I purposely didn't send you a text message about the meeting because there was no reason to. Coach Cal loves your work ethic, and everyone around this program respects the hard work you put in each day. We believe you can definitely help the team. We want you on campus at the start of school in August."

I left Martin's office with a smile on my face and a sigh of relief because of the huge burden that had been lifted from my shoulders. I had done it; I was going to be able to finish out my senior season. Of course, I was upset about my friends no longer being on the team, but, at the same time, I had worked hard for this tiny moment of glory.

My knees shook in excitement as I realized that things were starting to fall into place. A nationally ranked team, an electrifying season, and a uniform all awaited me in the fall.

As soon as I got outside, I called my mom and dad to tell them the exciting news. They were both ecstatic that I would be returning to the team. I hoped the news would lift my mom's spirits as she prepared to undergo her second spine surgery. I thought the news that I'd be back in uniform might just give her the extra strength she needed to pull through.

• • •

I wasted no time rushing back home to Newport to be with my mom before the operation. Even though the first surgery on her spinal cord a few months earlier had been successful, more tumors had formed, and cancer was now present inside the protective covering of her spinal cord. It was a dangerous and life-threatening situation.

It took much deliberation, but the surgeon finally decided to work on her. Even though it was a high-risk procedure, we knew it had to be done. Over the years, we'd grown accustomed to medical professionals shying away from such a complex patient like my mom, but she only saw it as a testament to how long she'd fought, and I did too.

On the day of her surgery, the family gathered at the hospital to once again witness the strength of my mom. We prayed her heart would withstand the effects of the anesthetic and her body would endure being cut wide open. We also had faith that when everything was finished, she would wake up, move her legs, and maybe even wiggle her toes.

I remember seeing my mom before they took her into the operating room. Andrew, Mandy, my dad, and I each gave her a big hug and kiss. She promised us she would make it out of the operation alive, and we all knew better than to doubt her.

I sat in the waiting room with my fingers crossed for what seemed like an eternity. Finally, after five long hours, we received word that the surgery was a success. Although she felt hints of nausea, my mom awoke with feeling in her extremities. She could make a fist and bend her legs. Needless to say, it was a huge relief to the entire family, and we couldn't wait for her to recover because we were confident her quality of life would be greatly improved.

> We had faith that when everything was finished she would wake up, move her legs, and maybe even wiggle her toes

# 11

# SUCCESS
## The Wildcats are Back

By the time August rolled around, I couldn't wait to get back to Lexington. Knowing my mom was safe at home and recovering definitely made moving back to school easier.

My senior year seemed different for obvious reasons. For one, it was only August, and the excitement for basketball season had already spread around campus, throughout Lexington, and across Kentucky. I tried to make time stand still because I knew the months were going to fly by, and I wanted to cherish every second, every moment. I wanted this year to last a lifetime.

To top it all off, August of 2009 meant Andrew was finally off to college. Because he'd chosen to attend UK, I pulled some strings to get him a spot in Wildcat Lodge. It put my mom's mind at ease knowing he was in good hands with me in Lexington, and living in the same dorm gave us an opportunity to bond as brothers. I took delight in the fact that I could be there to help him get through his first year of college.

• • •

The home stretch of my college career was shaping up nicely, and I couldn't wait to get started with basketball.

Coach Calipari started out the semester by holding individual meetings with each player. Not only did he want to get the 2009-2010 season started off on the right foot, he wanted to know where each of us was mentally. I eagerly waited my turn to meet with Coach because I wanted to finally thank him for allowing me to remain a part of the team. I was thrilled when Eric Bledsoe exited Coach's office because that meant I was up next.

After I settled in my chair, Coach Calipari took his seat across the table from me. Then he began to ask questions about the upcoming season. He wanted to know what a successful season looked like to me on a personal level and how I envisioned the outcome of the season in regards to the team. He also wanted to assess where I could fit into his system.

I talked for a few minutes about how I've wanted to win championships since the day I stepped on campus. I explained to him that I wanted to put in the work every single day to improve all aspects of my game. I also told him that my true value rested in the fact that I was willing to do anything necessary for the good of the team and that I had no personal agenda of any kind, except to win.

Coach then discussed what he wanted from me during the season, "Mark, I want you around because you can provide leadership to an inexperienced team. It's tough for you guys that have been here to deal with all the changes, but this year can be something special. I believe our team has a lot of depth. When I first got here, I couldn't believe some of the guys had a scholarship and you didn't. I think you can help our team simply through your example and work ethic. I want to see you in the gym trying to improve each day. You owe it to your teammates."

After listening to each word Coach Cal spoke to me, I thanked him for allowing me to continue on. Then I left his office feeling more than a little optimistic about my future.

• • •

Following the individual meetings, Coach gave us a few weeks to get acquainted with classes before beginning pre-season workouts. The night before we were set to begin, he called us all together to talk about what to expect. During this particular meeting, Coach Cal did a little more than that. Among his words about how excited he was for the upcoming season, he took my dream to another level.

In the middle of his talk about how excited he was to get the season underway, Coach Calipari informed the gathering of players and coaches that he was going to award me the final scholarship.

These are words I'll never forget. "I'm going to give the final scholarship to Mark Krebs. I really think he can play, and I think he can really help this team win games. People were discussing maybe we should give it to this guy or that guy, but after talking with Coach Robic, I decided he was more deserving than anybody."

I sat there stunned; my heart beat rapidly. I couldn't comprehend what I was hearing. It was the biggest honor I could ever receive. My teammates cheered, and those that were close enough congratulated me with a pat on the back or a soft punch in the arm. I wanted to cry and smile all at the same time. It was almost unbelievable to realize that all the hard work I'd put in over the past three years had finally paid off – literally. The realization of earning a scholarship at the highest level of college basketball during a season of so much hype and promise filled me with uncontrollable excitement. I would forever become indebted to Coach Calipari for the opportunity he granted me that night.

**They could focus their efforts on my mom, and that meant the world to me.**

I spent an emotional rest of the evening on the phone with my mom and dad, although I couldn't even begin to explain everything the scholarship meant to me. It eased the sting of school loans. It afforded me one year of being financially worry free. And it allowed me to help Andrew get through his first year of school. For at least a moment, my family wouldn't have to give us anything. They could focus their efforts on my mom, and that meant the world to me.

After I sat talking on the phone well into the early morning hours telling everyone I knew about the amazing news, it was time to get focused on my contributions to the team. With an athletic scholarship and high expectations for the upcoming season, I had work to do.

• • •

Coach Calipari's workouts and conditioning were difficult, but they were also reasonable. Unlike anything I had been through in the previous years, his workouts were competitive and fun from beginning to end. He wasn't out to break anybody or push us past our limits. The purpose of the drills was to improve our skills while gradually getting us into better basketball shape.

Coach Cal would always say, "We don't need to be in mid-season shape right now. It's only October. You keep playing as hard as you are right now, and you'll be in the best shape in the country."

That made perfect sense to me. Why tear down the players so early in the season? I understand instilling toughness in a team, but I believe toughness can be gained gradually over the course of time with each workout.

The only problem was that I couldn't seem to slow down the course of time. Days were passing by too fast, and, before I knew it, I was staring in the face of my final Big Blue Madness.

As we closed in on the kickoff of the season, I could clearly see the team coming together, and I couldn't wait for the chaos to begin. Witnessing thousands of fans camping outside for almost an entire week for Big Blue Madness tickets was awesome. Seeing the unyielding support for Kentucky Basketball that surrounded us influenced every player on the team. It was amazing to see how Coach Calipari and the anticipation for the new season drew more fans to camp out this year than the previous three years combined.

Without a question, Big Blue Madness is an electrifying event each and every October, but this year was different. It seemed like there was more passion and anticipation than any other year. The energy of the crowd, the loud cheering of my entire family, and the thought that the season was right around the corner created indescribable emotions in me.

When I was hoisted up into the rafters on a scissors lift to be introduced to the 23,000 screaming fans, I could barely hear my name being called. The cheers, the fireworks, and the music made it nearly impossible to even hear myself think. As I waved to the die-hard fans, I did my best to soak it all in. I wanted to remember the sights, sounds, and sensations of that moment forever. When the 2009-2010 Kentucky Wildcats and new head coach, John Calipari, were revealed to the jam-packed crowd at Rupp Arena, it was utter pandemonium.

As the night rolled on, fans were treated to the public debut of the John Wall Dance, numerous celebrities, and an unbelievable array of dunks. Player after player flew through the air toward the hoop, trying to outperform the previous dunk. The actual scrimmage even had the makings of a slam-dunk contest.

I couldn't begin to imagine what the regular season would be like after seeing the early practices and Big Blue Madness. The quickness, the athleticism, and the fun each of us was having on the court would surely be deadly for any opponent we faced. Only two weeks of practice stood between me and my final season with the Wildcats. It had the makings of a truly unforgettable year.

• • •

Needless to say, the extremely talented freshmen, as well as the rest of the team, lived up to the hype.

To get things rolling, John Wall hit the game-winning jumper against Miami (OH) in only the first official game of his career. He followed it up with game-winning plays against Stanford at the Cancun

Challenge and UCONN on the court at Madison Square Garden in New York City.

I honestly couldn't believe I'd finally made the trip to New York. It took two years, but I earned the right to experience the famous Madison Square Garden. After losing to Gardner Webb two years prior, I didn't think I'd ever get a chance to play there. Lucky for me, I was wrong. Not only was the game against UCONN a thrilling finish, but it was also just the game we needed to propel us on a spectacular winning streak.

Early on in the season, despite having so many close games, we always found a way to escape with a victory. We overwhelmed all of our opponents in the non-conference schedule, including UNC, Indiana, and Louisville. As a matter of fact, we won 19 straight games to begin the season and eventually earned a #1 ranking in the nation.

It was the ride of a lifetime to the top of the charts, and it was incredible to be part of the team that was bringing Kentucky back to prominence. Perhaps, the most important game of the early part of the season was when we became the first program nationally to reach 2,000 wins.

I played 10 minutes in the win against Drexel, and when the confetti fell from the rafters at Rupp Arena, a warm feeling filled my heart. Looking up at the retired jerseys that lined the top of the arena, I realized rather quickly that I was part of a truly remarkable tradition. Even though my four years were a rollercoaster ride, all the emotional and physical pain I experienced was well worth it.

Coach Calipari put it best, "Enough can't be said about the history of Kentucky Basketball, and all the people who accumulated so many wins. However, you guys can all take pride in the fact that this team carried it across the finish line, and all of Kentucky can be pleased about being the first to 2,000 wins."

The transformation my career had made in just one year was unbelievable. I was witnessing some particularly extraordinary events, meeting incredible people, and reaching enormous milestones. Coach

Calipari introduced us to many significant people and unique opportunities throughout the season. Not only did we raise nearly $1.5 million in relief efforts for earthquake-ravaged Haiti, but we also met a tremendous number of influential people on a daily basis. Superstar athletes like Magic Johnson and Lebron James, the owner of the New England Patriots, Robert Kraft, and rap musician, Drake, are only a few of the people we met that year. We even received a call from the President of the United States, Barack Obama.

• • •

It's truly amazing to gaze back over the 2009-2010 season because it creates such inspiration inside of me. The season filled me with a lifetime full of experiences even before I reached conference play. And that was just the beginning.

Throughout SEC play, we kept winning. Even though our 19-game winning streak came to an end at South Carolina, we didn't let it get us down. We stayed true to our course and marched on to become the SEC Regular Season Champion, with Tennessee as our only other loss.

We entered the game against Florida – Senior Day – with a record of 13 wins and 2 losses in conference play and a 28-2 record overall. It was the day I'd been looking forward to for a long time. When I found out Coach Calipari wanted me in the starting lineup against the Florida Gators, I crossed yet another accomplishment off my list.

I thought about what this day was going to mean for my family. It signified the culmination of a long journey. I was proud of how far I had come, but I was also devastated to think that I'd be playing my last game in Rupp Arena.

I talked to my mom early on in the day and made it clear to her that if she didn't feel up to making the trip I understood completely. She put my worries to rest when she assured me it would take an army to keep her from being at midcourt to share in the special moment. I knew from a long history of beating the odds that my mom would be there, no doubt about it.

After my conversation with her, I was ready to prepare for the game. But it was odd knowing I'd be getting dressed in our locker room for the last time. It was even stranger to realize that I'd be making my very last run out of the tunnel and onto the court at Rupp Arena.

Nonetheless, I was ready for the Senior Day festivities to begin. Even though I replayed how the day would turn out over and over in my head throughout my career, nothing could have prepared me.

As they lined each of the seniors up to be introduced, a flood of emotion overcame me. An unusual yet extraordinary feeling rushed through my body. When my name was finally announced, and I broke through the banner to see my family – Andrew, Mandy, Peyton, Dad, and Mom – all at center court, I nearly broke down in tears. I couldn't help but think back to the incredible journey I'd taken to get to this moment in my life.

I remembered being a water boy for my dad's high school team and thought about everything he'd taught me about the game of basketball. I thought about the beginning of my mom's diagnosis and the never-ending bad news that followed. My mind was filled with thoughts about my mom's amazing struggle to live, her battle against all odds, and my family's resilience. I thought about the chance I took leaving Thomas More, my rollercoaster ride at Kentucky through three coaches in only four years, and the sad truth that I would soon be playing my last game as a Wildcat in Rupp Arena. Above all else, I reflected on how much strength it took for my mom to be waiting there at half court to share in this special day with me. Just like my graduation from high school, she found the courage to be there, and that thought alone will put a smile on my face for as long as I live.

As I embraced my family at midcourt, I leaned down to kiss and hug my mom in her wheelchair. The cancer had grown so bad in her spine that she had become paralyzed from the waist down. Regardless of the fact that she was being wheeled everywhere she went, the energy it took for her to make the trip down to Lexington would wipe her out for days to follow. But according to her, it was energy well spent. As we hugged, I told her that I loved her, and that it meant a lot to me that she'd made it.

She whispered softly in my ear, "I promised you I would be here. I wouldn't have missed this for the world."

After we shot each other a smile, Coach Calipari presented me with a framed jersey. I held it up to show my gratitude to the 23,000 fans that had made my last four years a dream.

When Perry, Ramon, and Patrick finished their introductions, it was time for the traditional playing of "My Old Kentucky Home." While the music played, I looked around at each of the seniors and thought about the ride we'd been on since we stepped foot in Lexington. I glanced over at the rest of my teammates and thought about the incredible year we'd been blessed with. I fought back the emotions because I needed to start the game out on the right track. Above all else, I wanted to go out on top and leave Rupp Arena with a victory.

> ## Just as I'd imagined it so many times, Senior Day was a true success

I fought to stay focused and prepared, and when it came time for tip-off, I was more ready than I'd ever been before. When I left the game after about seven minutes of play, we were ahead and would keep the lead the entire game. Just as I'd imagined it so many times, Senior Day was a true success.

• • •

With Florida as the final game of the regular season, the 2010 SEC Tournament in Nashville, Tennessee, was right around the corner. The streets, bars, and arena were a sea of blue. As a team, we understood that the SEC Tournament was a vacation to most Kentucky fans, and with that in mind, we made the decision to play each game like it was our last.

After winning our first two games of the tournament against Alabama and Tennessee, we were set to face off Mississippi State in the final game.

The finals against Mississippi State will undoubtedly go down as one of the best finishes in the history of the tournament. We pulled out an overtime victory after a last-second put back by DeMarcus Cousins at the end of regulation. It was an amazing feeling to finally win the SEC Tournament.

As we held up the trophy in front of the sell-out crowd, I tried to imprint the moment in my memory. I let my senses take in all of my surroundings because I wanted to remember the feeling forever. The SEC Tournament turned out to be incredible, and the whole experience let me picture what winning the NCAA Tournament would be like. The thought gave me butterflies in my stomach.

Even though extreme jubilation followed the championship game, we didn't have much time to celebrate the victory. We had to be back in Lexington for the NCAA Tournament Selection Show that same night.

• • •

The players and staff piled into Coach Cal's living room, eager to find out where we'd be playing and who would be in our bracket.

After receiving the #1 seed in the East Region of the tournament, we found out we were set to play East Tennessee State University in New Orleans, LA. Every ounce of my being was filled with excitement about my first tournament appearance. I laughed inside at the thought of the NCAA Tournament two years prior and the news that I couldn't dress for the first-round game against Marquette. I thought about how much motivation that moment created inside of me. It propelled me to my current position: a scholarship player on a team looking for a national championship. It was surreal.

We ended the night with a meeting because Coach wanted to tell us what we were up against. Sitting around his basement, he spoke to the team about what to expect during the next couple of weeks.

He stated, "No one in here has ever scored in an NCAA Tournament game. Even though that's hard to believe, it's the truth. We all need to stay humble and hungry to have a chance to win this thing. Only take one game at a time because one slip up, and it's over. Throughout the years, I've seen that the team that's having the most fun usually wins the championship. So let's go out there and have a ball."

We took all of Coach's words to heart, and the first weekend in New Orleans started off with a bang.

We ran through ETSU thanks to Eric Bledsoe's barrage of record-setting three-pointers, and near the end of the game, I checked into the first NCAA Tournament game of my career. It was unbelievable that I'd finally dressed for the tournament, but actually playing in it was beyond words.

In my two minutes of play, I even got off a few shots. Unfortunately, none of them landed. In the locker room after the game, the guys gave me a hard time for missing, but just like always, I didn't care because we'd won. Kentucky was headed to the second round.

After Wake Forest upset Texas in the first round, they became our next opponent. Again, we ran through Wake Forest, and the further the game went along, the more I realized I was going to have a chance to redeem myself. When I went to check into the game, I thought about how this could be the last time I ever played. It was important that I make it memorable.

When I finally got my chance, the first three-pointer I shot rimmed out. The next time down the floor, their 7-foot big man in the middle threw my layup into the stands. I didn't lose faith, though. I hoped for one last shot attempt to end my career on a high note.

As I threw the ball inbounds, I followed the ball over to the right wing for a handoff. Once I caught it, I let a fall-away three-pointer fly with 19 seconds left on the clock. The ball seemed to travel through the air in slow motion. It felt good when I let it go, and it looked even better in flight. My teammates jumped through the roof when the ball went through the net. The arena in New Orleans erupted.

Backpedaling down the court, I smiled from ear to ear knowing my family, especially my mom, was back home in Newport cheering as loud as they could. The thought of her smiling at the television played in my mind. I could envision my aunts, uncles, cousins, and friends bursting out in celebration. It made me happy simply knowing the joy it brought them.

> **That, in itself, was and always will be a dream come true**

Just as my career had begun with a three-pointer at Rupp Arena, it ended, at least for the moment, with a three-pointer in the NCAA Tournament. That, in itself, was and always will be a dream come true.

# INSPIRATION
## Beyond the Dream

Sadly, after a Sweet Sixteen win against Cornell in the Carrier Dome, disaster struck as we fell in defeat against West Virginia University in the Elite Eight.

The 2009-2010 season wasn't just the end of a career for me, but the conclusion of an incredible dream. After the game against West Virginia, I didn't just say good-bye to basketball. No, I said good-bye to an intricate part of myself. The honeymoon was over. The very obsession that had served as a release from the harshness of real life was gone. Practices and games were no longer there to take my mind off the pressures and pain at home. My family no longer had the excitement of crowding around the television to cheer their Kentucky Wildcat on to victory.

After four years, the trips from Newport to Rupp Arena that had been like vacations from the everyday hardships of chemotherapy, doctor's appointments, and medical bills for my mom and family had come to a painful end. But even in such difficult times as these, I believed

> I believed in seeing the bright side in every situation

in seeing the bright side in every situation, the silver lining in every cloud, and the positive in every circumstance.

Even in the face of ache and defeat, I can't deny how truly blessed I am.

• • •

Looking back, my career was a part of the most turbulent time in the history of Kentucky Basketball. I played for three coaches in only four years, but, fortunately, through it all, I gained the gift of being able to adapt to any situation. In part, I am who I am today because of each of my college coaches.

I consider myself tremendously lucky to have had my career begin under Coach Tubby Smith. He is a man of great integrity and character, a leader with unyielding qualities. He took a chance and gave me the opportunity of a lifetime. He saw what I could offer the team, not who I knew or where I came from.

In the same manner, Coach Gillispie was gracious enough to give a red-shirt walk-on like myself the chance to prove himself worthy of another opportunity. Down to his core, he strived every day to make not only better basketball players but also better men. Even though his methods were unusual, his goal was for us to reach far beyond our limits, and through that goal, he taught me the value of hard work.

But it was Coach Calipari who brought the winning atmosphere and fun back to the University of Kentucky. Not only did he allow me the chance to finish out my senior season, he also awarded me a scholarship. For that, I will always be grateful. His charisma, heart, and energy are infectious, and when combined with his vast knowledge of the game, it makes for a powerful combination.

Every coach I've had since I was young played their part in molding me as an individual, but my family has by far had the biggest influence. My mother's battle and my family's collective fight have given me a unique outlook on life.

• • •

Unfortunately, I have seen firsthand the fragility of life and how short it can be, but it remains essential for me to have an optimistic attitude even when there seems to be no end in sight. When you're a freshman in high school and you witness a disease take a tremendous toll on the very person who gave you life, it forces you to stay positive. That experience and all those that followed it, instilled in me the persistence to stay on course regardless of the obstacles in my path. Taking my mom's lead, I never allowed myself to sweat the small stuff. Although cancer is always on our minds at home, we refuse to let it consume us. My mom encourages us all to lead normal, happy lives. She gives testament to living for the joy of life, not for the sorrow of cancer.

There is no medical reason why my mom has survived these last nine years; there's no reason at all except to say that the Man upstairs must recognize and embrace a beautiful life when He sees it.

No matter what new nurse walks through the door to assist Mom's chemo for that week, the reaction is always the same. My mom finds humor in the fact that they look at her chart, look at her, stare at her chart, and then continue to scan her up and down trying to figure out how she's still sitting there alive.

I don't think it's a mystery, though. If you spent any time with her at all, you'd quickly realize that she has her heart set on a multitude of goals, and not even cancer can divert her away from them. Although she has reached most of her milestone-marking goals like seeing Andrew graduate from high school, me step onto the court for the University of Kentucky, and Mandy get married, she continues to face her daily fight by focusing on the goals she sets for herself, even if they are a little more simplistic now. At the top of her list are being strong enough to go on a family vacation, waking up each day to share a laugh with her family, and living another day to hear the pitter-patter of her granddaughter's feet as she scampers around the house.

My mom once told me that she doesn't believe in miracles, she depends on them. Thanks to her awe-inspiring courage and faith, I, too, am a firm believer that having a strong faith allows all the other aspects of life to fall into place. A big reason why she far exceeded the timeframe of living only nine months is that she began to worry about others far more than she worried about herself. No one would have faulted her for wallowing in her own self-pity, but she didn't allow herself to do that.

Coach Calipari always said, "The more you care about your teammates, the easier life is on you."

My mom truly exemplifies these words. No matter what she goes through, other people's problems, regardless of how small they are, are always more important than her own.

• • •

I must admit that it took an extensive process to get to the point where we are as a family today. There was a time when we cursed the thought of cancer. A time when we spent our days wondering, "Why our family?"

In the fall of my sophomore year at Newport Central Catholic, a teacher approached me to speak at a Thanksgiving celebration we were having at school. Holding a grudge at the situation my mom found herself in, I immediately declined the opportunity to speak about all I was thankful for. What was I thankful for? Why did God choose my mom to have this cruel disease? Why, for the last year, had my life been flipped and turned upside down? As I searched for answers to these questions, I overlooked the treasures that were right in front of me.

When I finally ceased feeling sorry for myself, I began to realize everything I should be grateful for. Thoughts of everyone who had lent a helping hand to our family flashed in my mind. My heart started to feel unburdened as I remembered the fundraisers and the never-ending storm of food that found itself at our doorstep. I felt warmth knowing that we were given the opportunity to find out who our friends truly are. I felt strength thinking about how close my family had grown.

I found myself up there on the podium that Thanksgiving in front of the school because I understood there was a great deal to be thankful for. It was my job to shine a light on the kind people with extremely large hearts who are always there to give unconditionally to those around them. After all, isn't that what life's all about?

・・・

Even today, despite the pain cancer continues to cause my mom, I try to envision the undeniable good that has come from such a dreadful experience. I find myself in a debt of gratitude to my family for all they have done. I think back to when I decided to go to UK, and the only reason I was able to pursue my dream in the first place was because of my family's incredible resilience. I felt comfort in the fact that my dad, my siblings, my aunts, and my uncles were at home doing anything necessary for the well-being of my mom. My mind was at ease knowing she was in good hands. It gave me the strength to let go a little, and it allowed me the opportunity to devote time to my teammates.

I think about those teammates I was able to meet and the brotherhood we formed over the years. It's an extremely unique kind of brotherhood – one built on grounds of diversity. Our huddle-breaking chants of "family" and "brothers" have never rung more true than they do now. My teammates, regardless of the race or color, are a part of my family now.

It never ceases to amaze me how people from all over the world can come together to establish a common vision, believe in a common dream, and accomplish a common goal. The moment we put on our uniforms, young men from New York City to Chicago, Detroit to Alabama, Louisiana to Alaska, California to Poland, and everywhere in between became Wildcats.

I reflect on the experiences I have shared with my teammates and realize a funny thing about sports. People always say it's only a game, but I tend to think a bit differently. I believe it can be a channel through which we as players have a greater effect on society. When

> # My mother's fight with cancer should exude inspiration

used correctly, it can be a vehicle to take you to destinations you never thought possible, an elevator to heights you never thought you could reach. Sports have been a significant part of my life, and I stand as proof that they can lead you to places you never thought you'd go and to people you never imagined you'd meet.

• • •

I find myself pleased when I look back at my journey to this point in my life. By no means should my mother's fight with cancer go down as a story of sadness; rather it should exude inspiration.

The past has led me to a distinctive realization: that it's in the trials and tribulations, the ups and the downs, that our character is created; that we learn the most about ourselves in how we overcome the low points in life; and that sometimes it's during the journey on the way to reaching our dreams that we discover the most about who we are and who we want to become.

> # ...beyond every obstacle there's hope and behind every dream there's a story

Take it from me, life is so much more wonderful when you embrace every day as a gift. It's important to remember that beyond every obstacle there's hope and behind every dream there's a story.